Coming of Age

With love, to my sisters, Yan Chi and Sheila, who never take their brother too seriously.

Coming of Age

An Exploration of Christianity and the New Age

Martin Palmer

Aquarian/Thorsons
An Imprint of HarperCollins*Publishers*

The Aquarian Press
An Imprint of HarperCollins*Publishers*
77-85 Fulham Palace Road,
Hammersmith, London W6 8JB

Published by The Aquarian Press 1993
1   3   5   7   9   10   8   6   4   2

A catalogue record for this book
is available from the British Library

ISBN 1 85538 229 6

Typeset by Harper Phototypesetters Limited,
Northampton, England
Printed in Great Britain by
Mackays of Chatham, Kent

Contents

Preface   7

1   What is the New Age?   15

2   New Age or New Revival?   29

3   Christ, the Antichrist and All Things New   59

4   Just Because They Are Dead, Doesn't
        Mean They Are Right   91

5   Body, Mind and Human Potential   113

6   Reimagining Society   133

7   'Behold I Make All Things New'   169

Notes   193

Bibliography   199

Index   203

Preface

I think I was asked to write this book because, in some sections of the Church and media, I am seen and named as a 'New Ager' or 'New Age Guru'. Yet there is probably no stronger a critic of much of what is called 'New Age' than myself. A bit of a contradiction! So I want to start by setting out my own position: a position from which I am both attracted and appalled by much of what is called the 'New Age', and by what is called Christianity.

I suppose it is my maternal grandfather who causes problems for me with the term New Age. I know very little about my grandfather for he disappeared from my grandmother and mother's lives just before the Second World War. But what little I know and have been told over the years since I was a boy has made me interested in him. He was an exceptionally brave man: he was a pacifist in the First World War, worked in the front lines for the Quaker Ambulance Brigade and was awarded one of Belgium's top medals for bravery. He was also a professional numerologist. That is to say, he travelled the country giving lectures on the mystical significance of numbers. He gave readings and taught classes which supposedly enabled people to determine their fortune according to the letters and therefore numbers in their names, or in the Bible. Had he lived today, his lectures, his writings, indeed his very work would have earned him the title of New Ager.

That is where the problem comes. As a child, I was fascinated by the little I could glean about him and his beliefs. I recall my grandmother taking me on one side, very secretly, and telling me that my name was a most powerful combination of numbers which meant that I would succeed at anything I ever tried. As a fourteen-year-old, I was all ears!

Ultimately, however, I saw my grandfather's work as being some strange, albeit intriguing, hangover from a discredited superstitious past. Wonderful fun and probably quite harmless, but in the final analysis pointless and with nothing 'new' about it.

I grew up in a Christian household, where faith was debated openly and disagreements seen as a sign of a healthy outlook. Religion was valued but not always taken too seriously. I was brought up in Anglican vicarages, but always in ecumenical parishes where the different churches tried to work together, and in such a context my grandfather's teachings were seen as irrelevant. Yet I always had a deep fascination for anything which smacked of the strange, odd or different in the world of faith, an interest which reflected not so much a personal quest as antiquarian interest.

It was out of antiquarian interest that I used to go looking for the Spiritualist Assemblies in the area in which I lived in as a teenager: the town of Swindon in North Wiltshire, Southern England. Like that much more interesting seventeenth-century resident of North Wiltshire, John Aubrey – antiquarian, gossip and inveterate writer and recorder – I was attracted to the remains of old superstitions and customs which lay almost hidden around me. I walked the hills of the Marlborough Downs with elderly gentlemen striding out the ley lines; I watched middle-aged women casting fortunes or reading crystal balls; I cycled to the great stone circles and ceremonial avenues of Avebury, between 3000 and 4000 years old, and the equally ancient and as yet unexplained vast man-made Silbury Hill, hoping to catch those very romantic Victorian-inspired Druids going about their rituals; I went out with ghost hunters tracking the spirits that haunted graveyards or that communicated through walls; I joined in seances and studied spirit writings. To me this was all part of a world that was fading before my eyes, one I found fascinating in the extreme. It was largely ignored by all around me, and indeed I felt for those who were so ignored. I had grown up until the age of fourteen on a vast postwar housing estate on the edge of the city of Bristol in the South West of England, where the Church itself represented a threatened form of spirituality. I can recall quite distinctly believing that by the turn of the century, even the Church would have ceased to exist. It was very hard, living where I lived, to believe that anyone was interested in the spiritual, religious world. In the early 1960s, science was still held in great reverence and was thought to be rolling back the frontiers of the universe to reveal nothing beyond. Secularism was the way of the future and Christianity – indeed any form of religion – was merely a remnant from the past.

Had it been possible for me to be catapulted forward from, say, 1966 to the 1990s, I think I would have been most surprised by the resurgence of interest in all things spiritual, mystical, magical and religious – it is perhaps worth remembering how great this increase in interest is. As for myself, much of what is called New Age simply reminds me of the quaint old practices that were to be found around me, if one looked hard enough, as a child. Most of all I think of my grandfather, picturing him from the few photographs I have seen of him: dressed in good but standard 1920s suits, here is the numerologist, the archetypal New Ager, not living it up in California, USA but dwelling in Leamington Spa, England, so long ago.

I also have difficulty with the term New Age because I have often been described, by those who oppose the work I and my colleagues do, as a New Ager. I am part of an organization with the instantly forgettable title of the International Consultancy on Religion, Education and Culture – ICOREC. Consultants are drawn from all the major faiths of the world and represent a wide cross-section within each faith. ICOREC has consultants in countries around the world as well as a home team based in the United Kingdom, and particularly at its Manchester headquarters.

The consultancy's working principle is that each faith should speak for itself in all the work that we undertake, but in a way that is accessible to others and bears in mind the audience that it is addressing. We intend that faith should speak to faith, and also that the faiths should speak to the secular world and to education.

Central to our work is the idea that religion and beliefs play a key role in shaping and giving meaning to our daily lives and the ways in which we perceive and value the world around us. To this end we deal with religion at the day-to-day level as well as at the philosophical and conceptual level, seeking always to acknowledge the diversity of ways in which religion and belief affect us.

Part of my work in ICOREC is to be adviser to HRH

the Prince Philip, Duke of Edinburgh in his capacity as President of the World Wide Fund for Nature International (WWF). The places and events to which we have taken Prince Philip have seemed to fascinate the media and have led to me being described as his 'guru'. Needless to say, this is not the case! Our work has upset some people who believe either that working with the different faiths is in some way betraying Christianity; or who feel concern for the environment is equivalent to paganism or pantheism. As our team includes, for example, Muslims, Hindus and Jews, I as a practising Christian have been particularly singled out for vilification. It is in this context that I have sometimes been termed a New Age person - or, as the secular press would have it, a New Age guru.

Although I could be described as the grandson of a New Ager, I have to confess that I do not feel that I warrant the term. I am fascinated for all sorts of reasons with the ideas, materials and questions arising within the new era of spirituality. I believe there are profoundly important things coming from and being raised by this latest religious revival, and I would confess that I have been much changed by my encounter with some of the ideas and groups that are lumped together - often by publishers and the media - under the term the New Age, which term I shall try to define in Chapter 1. But in the end I find that the Christian faith still makes more sense of the world and of me than anything else I have encountered. Having said that, I would have to acknowledge that my understanding of Christianity is not what might be described as conventional Anglicanism. I find myself as distressed, angered, challenged and frustrated by much of Christianity as by much of the New Age. I am an unconventional but devout Anglican - but I am not sure that I qualify for the title of New Ager.

When I was a boy, exploring the mysterious world which lay around me, I often used to visit the rather dingy second-hand bookshops of old Bristol. Here, in gently mouldering rooms, musty with the smell of damp, dusty, unwanted books, I would hunt out those sections likely to contain books on areas such as numerology, the occult, ley lines, magic or the ancient Egyptian Book of the Dead. To do this, you had to look for labels saying something like 'Religion', 'Spiritualism', 'Occult', or 'Eastern Thought'. Here, amidst piles of Madam Blavatsky, the nineteenth-century spiritualist, or the 1934 Year Book of the Society for Psychical Research, I could find gems awaiting me: hardback books with marvellous drawings, diagrams, faded photographs or even occasionally lithographs, on everything from the 'superstitions' of the pygmies to unsolved mysteries of Britain, endless books decoding the pyramids or Stonehenge and accounts of how the Book of Revelation was coming true TODAY (usually printed in the late 1880s).

My point is a simple one. In the 1960s, I never went looking for this material in ordinary bookshops. There was very little there. It was the province of the second-hand bookshops to hold the stock of what would now be called New Age books. There were certainly presses producing interesting material, but they were small and their output scattered, one problem being that proper bookshops didn't know under which heading to classify this material.

Today, the situation is very different, for many ordinary bookshops now have sections into which these books will go. The sections vary in title - 'Alternative Philosophies', 'New Age', 'Occult and Magic' - but they

all make space for the vast array of titles pouring out of
even the most staid of publishing houses. For to a certain
extent, the phenomenon of the New Age is a publishing
phenomenon, in part created, certainly sustained and
possibly even at times invented by a publishing world
that has sensed the spiritual and religious hunger and has
set out to make money feeding it. As we shall see, this
is nothing new. All spiritual revivals in the West since the
early sixteenth century have been accompanied, to some
extent taken over by and certainly profited from by
publishers.

In this book, I want to look critically at many of the
claims and counter-claims being made about both the
New Age and, to a certain degree, Christianity. I want to
explore the fact that every generation faced by stressful
social, economic, cultural and spiritual challenges has
believed this must be a harbinger of a new age. I want to
investigate to what extent the ideas and models lumped
together under the label New Age are rooted not just in
the mindset of the West, albeit spiced up with titbits
from the Eastern religions, but also in certain
understandings of Christianity. Then, by looking at some
of the extraordinary outpourings of those evangelical and
fundamentalist Christians who want to believe in a New
Age Movement of Satanic hue, I want to show how wrong
some forms of Christianity can be. In the last three
chapters, I want to look at some of the very important
issues, ways of thinking and questions that are emerging
from the new interactions between body, mind, and
spirit, between religion and science and between faiths.
Finally, I want to posit the radical changes that
Christianity needs to make within itself; the new way of
visioning the world and the movements already
underway which might mean a dramatically re-viewed

Christianity plays a significant role in the community of faiths and beliefs of the future. For I believe there is a new form of Christianity arising.

Chapter 1

What is the New Age?

There is a major upsurge in religious and spiritual interest and activity in the Western world. New religious groups emerge weekly; books on spiritual issues sell in vast quantities; science is entertaining the idea that there are links between physics and metaphysics. The West is in the grips of what is effectively a religious revival. But unlike past revivals, the churches have little to do with it. Indeed, some churches see Satan, not God as being the source behind this upsurge. Others in the churches realize that contemporary Western society is looking for a new spiritual centre and is not looking to Christianity. This leads such churches to ask, what is wrong with our message or content? These are challenging times. Demonic or godly, the upsurge is producing some fascinating, alarming, silly and profound movements and groups. So what is going on?

Before looking in detail at what sort of movement or movements the New Age is, and at its roots and parallels in history, I want to try to make some sort of working definition of what the New Age is, and what it is not. Easier said than done, for the New Age is quintessentially a blanket term, though some try to use it more specifically. So is it possible to give a definition of what is meant by New Age? What is New about the New Age, and does the term actually mean anything?

Ironically, one of the main features of what is termed the New Age is that it is not at all new. Its roots lie back in the ancient past. They are found in pre-Christian myths and ideas, or sometimes in fanciful reinventions of a pre-Christian past. The roots stretch back to ancient Egypt and over the Great Wall into the Taoist China of the past. Much of what is today gathered together under the name of the New Age is in fact an at times exciting, at times thought-provoking, at times highly imaginative explor-ation of the past and its spiritual traditions and insights. Far from being new, much of the material to be found lumped together under the term New Age is very, very old.

What is new are the configurations into which some of this ancient material is put, the issues which it is asked to address and the new models of reality which occasionally burst forth from this varied mass. For many, discovery of these ancient teachings or ideas is all part of the coming of a new age which is either upon us of just about to burst upon us. The belief that the old world or age is passing away and a new age is dawning is as old as time itself. Yet it is this belief above all others, this conviction that a new era has dawned, foretold by the sages, which seems to mark out those who wish to call themselves New Age. It finds echoes in, indeed, is rooted in biblical and Christian ideas, some of which are highly destructive and dangerous, as I hope to show later.

It would be instructive to begin by looking at some of the different ways those within the New Age, those on the edge and those well outside it view its meaning and significance.

The View from Within

One of the best overall descriptions of the New Age comes from Eileen Campbell:

'New Age' is an umbrella term, but as with all such general terms it has both advantages and disadvantages. It is a useful term because it describes an emerging world-view, but it is occasionally meaningless in so far as it has been exploited to include some weird and dubious activities. Usually 'New Age' is used to denote a whole range of interests including health and well-being, the many forms of therapy or self-help, the practice of an esoteric or spiritual tradition, concern for the rest of humanity and the environment, and respect for Nature and feminine wisdom.[1]

It is this idea of an 'emerging world-view' that is really at the heart of many people's excitement about the New Age. But what exactly is meant by this? One of the great classics of the New Age is Marilyn Ferguson's *The Aquarian Conspiracy* (1980). At the end of her book she describes a 'New Mind, New World':

We have had a profound paradigm shift about the Whole Earth. We know it now as a jewel in space, a fragile water planet. And we have seen that it has no natural borders. It is not the globe of our school days with its many coloured nations . . . .

We are learning to approach problems differently, knowing that most of the world's crises grew out of the old paradigm – the forms, structures and beliefs of an obsolete understanding of reality. Now we can seek answers outside the old frameworks, ask new questions, synthesize and imagine.[2]

This statement by Ferguson captures what the 'emerging world-view' is seen to consist of. A discovery that the old certainties and models are no longer certain or even valid. A belief that by thinking anew, the world is made anew and thus problems are solved. It is the core belief of many within the New Age, and beyond it, that by changing the way we see things, we can then solve the problems that appeared insoluble when viewed through the glasses of the old model.

This is not exactly new. Every new ideology or belief system has taught this in one form or another. Otherwise, why would people have 'converted' to an alien or new world vision such as that offered by the Buddha to the tired early Hinduism of his time; or to Christianity in the midst of the vast array of deities and faiths of the Roman Empire; or to Marxism, which spoke so clearly and powerfully to the oppressed working classes of the cities of Europe in the late nineteenth century?

In that sense, the 'emerging world-view' of the New Age has an honourable heritage and may well mark as fundamental a shift in attitudes and behaviour as the other examples cited above created in their time, and create to this day.

At times, those writing about the New Age from within make it sound like nothing more than a revital- ization of certain beliefs and traditions which have become lost over time and through the accretion of cultural glosses to the words or actions of the religious teachers. Thus David Spangler, formerly of the Findhorn Community in north-east Scotland – one of the original centres of New Age thinking - says this of the New Age:

The New Age is essentially a symbol representing the
human heart and intellect in partnership with God
building a better world that can celebrate values of
community, wholeness and sacredness. It is a symbol
for the emergence of social behaviour based on a
worldview that stimulates creativity, discipline,
abundance and wholeness; it is a symbol for a more
mature and unobstructed expression of the sacredness
and love at the heart of life. It has very little to do
with the emergence of psychic phenomena. [3]

This sounds like the sort of statement that just about any
religious organization could turn out to justify their
actions. But Spangler goes on to give a much more
exciting picture:

The New Age represents social, political, economic,
psychological and spiritual efforts to recognise and
include all that our modern society has tended to
exclude: the poor, the dispossessed, the feminine,
the ecological and inwardly, all the painful repressed
and unintegrated material that Carl Jung called
the shadow. [4]

Here is a picture which does take us into a promise of
the beginnings of new territory. Whilst in the past,
various faiths and belief systems may in fact have dealt
with many if not all of the above, Spangler claims that
never before has there been such a conscious attempt to
do this and to do so within the context of the spiritual
question of 'the human heart and intellect in partnership
with God'. I'm afraid that, having looked long and hard,

I see little evidence of this in what calls itself the New Age. I do see all the major religious traditions of the world doing this in a way which would have been considered inconceivable fifty years ago, but they do so from their own religious roots, not through some New Age movement.

Spangler also gives an important clue to one aspect of the self-understanding of the New Age in *Revelation - Birth of the New Age*. Spangler sees the New Age as part of an evolutionary development of the human being and in particular of the human mind. The idea of such an evolution, which implies that humanity is becoming more and more mature, is first found explicitly in the writings of Teilhard de Chardin. Teilhard de Chardin (1881-1955) was a French Jesuit priest whose area of special expertise was evolution, archeology, palaeontology and philosophy. In his writings he portrayed humanity as evolving both physically and mentally and as a result he believed that the future for the human race could only go on improving as we learnt from our past and expanded our ability to understand and control the present and the future. Teilhard's views have had a profound effect on the New Age way of self-understanding and we shall return to them later.

Spangler is very much in tune with Teilhard's thinking when he says:

This New Age has been foreseen for centuries by individuals who had learned to manifest a cosmic consciousness and could witness, freed from time and space, the unfolding patterns of development for life on this planet. They saw that this New Age would bring as the logical continuance of the unfolding of creative being, an important phase in the curriculum of consciousness. They also saw that prior development and preparation would be needed by evolving life, humanity in particularly, in order properly to receive and benefit from the energies and opportunities the New Age would bring. With this knowledge, these great ones began to prepare the consciousness of mankind [sic] and of all the world.[5]

This belief that our time is the fulfilment and culmination of all that has gone before is of course logical at one level, but it is also eternal. As we shall see, every time there has been a great spiritual upheaval, people have seen their time foretold by those who came before them. Indeed, the whole of St Matthew's Gospel is founded upon just such an idea as that expressed by Spangler.

Another feature of the New Age's self-definition is its catholicity. It is seen by both those within and those well outside it, as having its influence in almost all areas of human life and thought. It is not a term that is used just to describe the young or way-out. Indeed, usually when I am being described as a New Ager it is in association with HRH Prince Philip with whom I work at times. Any movement which can have Prince Philip cited as an example alongside California channellers of millennium-old warriors, has to be fairly catholic!

In 1976, before the term New Age was in common use, Ferguson published an editorial in her newsletter *Brain/Mind Bulletin* in which she said:

Something remarkable is underway. It is moving with almost dizzying speed, but it has no name and eludes description . . . .

The spirit of our age is fraught with paradox. It is

at the same time pragmatic and transcendental. It
values both enlightenment and mystery . . . power
and humility . . . interdependence and individuality.
It is simultaneously political and apolitical. Its
movers and shakers include individuals who are
impeccably Establishment allied with one-time sign-
carrying radicals.

Within recent history 'it' has infected medicine,
education, social science, hard science, even
government with its implications. It is characterised
by fluid organisations reluctant to create hierarchical
structures, averse to dogma. It operates on the
principle that change can only be facilitated, not
decreed. It is short of manifestos. It seems to speak to
something very old. And, perhaps, by integrating
magic and science, art and technology, it will succeed
where all the King's horses and all the King's men
failed.[6]

That which Ferguson was unable to name in 1976,
indeed, even in 1980 she was not calling it New Age, is
one of the main strands of New Age thinking. The
networking, contacts, informal linking and overall sense
that things either are or can or should change, are all
hallmarks of what people both inside and outside the
New Age see as being typical of the New Age approach.
Indeed, many outside the New Age would recognize and
welcome just such movements, often taking place within
structures of which they are a part. Not all, by any means,
would use the term New Age of themselves, and we have
to be careful of allowing enthusiasts in the New Age from
co-opting such wider or more diverse movements.
However, it remains true that in the New Age view of
reality, such movements, even outside the official 'New

Age' are seen as confirmation of the validity of the New Age beliefs.

One of the core books of the New Age is Fritjof Capra's *The Tao of Physics*. First published in 1975, it explores the fascinating interrelationship between modern physics and ancient wisdom, especially that from the East. In words which pick up on Ferguson's thoughts at almost exactly the same time, Capra says:

For those who have experienced this harmony, the significance of the parallels between the world views of physicists and mystics is beyond any doubt. The interesting question, then, is not whether these parallels exist, but why; and furthermore, what their existence implies.[7]

As I said a little earlier, what is fascinating about the New Age at its best is the way in which it brings together parts of our cultures, parts of our knowledge and experience and fuses them together again. From this interaction comes a new way, or possibly, a renewed way of understanding and of relating to the world and to ourselves which is not only rooted and knowledgeable, but also innovative and challenging.

It is obvious from the quotations from both Campbell and Spangler that even those at the forefront of the movement see some of the activities which have accrued to the name New Age as undesirable or dubious. It will be important as we look at the nature of the New Age to bear that in mind, for at times the very openness and uncritical nature of much of the New Age leave it vulnerable to being used and exploited by the fools, liars and frauds of the religious world - of which there are many - both inside the New Age and outside in the major faiths.

The View from Without

I mention this because I now want to look at some of the views of those outside the New Age. The New Age is often seen by those outside as a much more cohesive and directed body than anyone inside the New Age could ever recognize. In part this emerges from the traditional, time-honoured way of dealing with new movements which you do not understand. You lump them all together and proclaim that they are an organized conspiracy.

The most famous, some would say infamous, attacks on the New Age come from the imaginative and highly successful best-seller writer, Constance Cumbey. Her *The Hidden Dangers of the Rainbow*, subtitled *The New Age Movement and our Coming Age of Barbarism*, takes conspiracy theory to its extreme, but her influence amongst both fundamentalists and others rigidly opposed to the New Age is disturbing. Her opening paragraphs leave the reader with little doubt as to where she stands:

It is the contention of this writer that for the first time in history there is a viable movement – the New Age Movement – that truly meets all the scriptural requirements for the antichrist and the political movement that will bring him on the world scene.

It is further the position of the writer that this most likely is the great apostacy or 'falling away' spoken of by the Apostle Paul and that the antichrist's appearance could be a very real event in our immediate future.[8]

A somewhat different interpretation of events leading to this movement from that offered by Spangler!

In Chapter 3 I explore the attitudes of Cumbey and others from the evangelical and fundamentalist wings of Christianity, but it is worth noting here that it is these sorts of groups who seem most convinced that they know exactly what the New Age is.

I have to say that I find no evidence of either a Movement which can be honestly titled New Age, or a conspiracy which can be called New Age. What I see are some very different and diverse activities going on, to which people from all walks of life and beliefs come for a host of different and often conflicting reasons, and which certain people then seize on and claim are signs of a mass movement. For instance, Ferguson cites yoga groups as a sign of the New Age in that people are seeking a new paradigm for their well-being. Yet people attend yoga groups for such a vast array of different reasons - back problems; stress; catholic interest in meditation; because a friend goes; hopes for a better sex life; health concerns; so as to do better in their job, and so on - that it is pure fantasy to say they are part, willingly or otherwise, of a mass movement, seeking and creating a new paradigm.

I would reiterate that the New Age is in part a publishing invention, for it has enabled publishers to lump together books and topics which otherwise would be very hard to market, namely, most of the esoteric, mystical, innovative and downright weird material which has been largely hidden in back streets, odd little magazines and such like for hundreds of years. Likewise, much of the hype of a New Age has been produced by packagers of events like Mind-Body-Spirit festivals or happenings like the Glastonbury Festival in Britain or the Harmonic Convergence in the USA. There are some people who wish to convince us that we are all on the

edge of a new age or new world, but as I shall attempt
to show later this is nothing new. What I find most
difficult about the claims of the New Age people who see
a Movement taking shape is that the evidence of people
and activities they cite is contradictory; those involved
often take great exception to being interpreted in this way
and the New Agers have a very bad habit of simply
naming anything they like New Age, regardless of what
the actual group or individuals, whom they have
incorporated into their Movement, see themselves as
doing or being.

Leading the Field?

If there is a mass movement abroad these days, not just
in California, the USA as a whole or Western Europe, but
worldwide then it is Islam. Yet the New Age simply
cannot handle Islam, except in its mystical Sufi
manifestations. It is the rise of renewed Islam that is
having the most powerful effect on the world,
challenging everything from Western science, political
theory, economics, the idea of human rights and the role
of education in a way which is affecting far more lives
than rebirthing groups, ideas of one world religion or
yoga sessions. New paradigms - or perhaps it would be
best to say, old paradigms renewed - are emerging from
Islam in astonishing profusion. Second only to Islam is
Christianity's own host of new ways of being Christian:
liberation theology, feminist theology, ecological
theology, new liturgies and so forth. Again, the vast
majority of the New Age has made no attempt to deal
with renewed and intellectual Christianity. The silence
of the New Age on anything to do with Islam shows the

very Western-oriented nature of its world-view, for all that it likes to claim that it is Eastern; similarly, the virtual silence on anything Christian other than selected mystics or gnosticism illustrates the inability of the New Agers to deal with realities that don't fit comfortably into their own model, in which they are the pacemakers.

The Challenge of Diversity

I simply do not see evidence of a New Age Movement. I do see evidence of a small and eclectic group of people who bunch together, for a vastly different array of reasons, under the title New Age. Thus in this book I shall use the term New Age primarily to describe such people. I shall also be looking at the one group which does genuinely believe the New Age exists - fundamentalist Christians, who want an enemy. As I hope to show, the two sides actually need to believe in each other in order to have something to be against. I do believe there are some exciting new ways of exploring and describing reality being posited at present. I believe there are massive challenges to human self-understanding and indeed to the question of the survival of the human race. But these are issues that are being addressed by many groups from many different backgrounds and for many different reasons. Simply because they express concern about the environment, for example, does not mean they are New Age. Far from it.

So I would argue that while some people find it helpful to use the term New Age to hold all these different views together, in doing so they actually stifle diversity, for reasons which will become clearer later in the book. For the vast majority of people, being called New Age is meaningless, whereas grappling with some of the issues now often associated with the New Age is vital. It is this dynamic which I hope to explore.

Chapter 2

New Age or New Revival?

It is the very nature of human use of the past that we believe that our own age, our own generation is at a point of summation or fulfilment of all that has gone before. We tend to read history aetiologically: that is, we project into the past explanations and causes for what is happening now or where we think we should be going. There is nothing distinctive about the current generation thinking that now is a new age. Let me illustrate this, for it is important to realize that much of the hype about a New Age is exactly that, and we are very arrogant if we think that ours is the only age to have had this vision and sense of excitement.

Biblical Precedents

The sense of standing on the edge of a New Age is first found clearly within the Bible, and in particular within the Book of Daniel. In his visions of the four beasts or empires of the world's history, Daniel saw his age as being the time when the worst such empire or beast would arise and would come to dominate, but that when this empire was at its height, then it would fall and a new age of God's direct, divine rule would supersede it and all would be well. In Daniel's vision, terrible warfare and violence precede the new age, because he interpreted history through a mixture of Jewish and Babylonian ideas. For Daniel the world consisted of two powerful forces: good and evil. Daniel could see these two forces at battle throughout history and he foresaw only struggle and pain until eventually the evil forces would be overthrown by God himself. This dualistic understanding of the world was new to Judaism; it came from the Jews' time of exile in Babylon, and it deeply affected and coloured much of their subsequent thinking.

The Book of Daniel purports to have been written during the Babylonian exile (587–c520 BC) but was in fact written when the Jews were fighting for their very existence against the armies of the Seleucid Greek king, Antiochus Epiphanes in the mid-second century BC. Out of warfare and violent struggle against a foe which desecrated the Temple and had expressed its intention of eradicating religious Judaism, Daniel interpreted history in terms of the struggle of good versus evil.

This tradition was carried on by the Book of Revelation, which nearly didn't make it into the final canon of the New Testament. It was opposed by many churches and in the Ethiopian Bible it is still often not included, nor does it have a position of honour in some of the Eastern churches. It made it in because of its association (almost certainly incorrect) with the beloved disciple of Jesus, John. It is a disturbing book, for much of what it teaches goes against the core of the Gospels themselves. It too sees the world and history as a series of struggles between good and evil which will culminate in violent warfare when the antichrist comes to rule the earth. Then, amidst horrors and abuses such as the world has never seen, Christ will return to earth and destroy the evil ones, Satan and his forces and inaugurate the heavenly kingdom, at which point peace will reign over all the earth. To the writer and to many early Christians, this new age of the kingdom was literally just around the corner. Christians bore the persecutions of the Roman Empire with great courage because they interpreted these trials as signs that the antichrist had come and that these were the final days before the glorious new age.

It is very ironic that these two books, with their visions of the forces of evil arising to previously unheard of powers immediately prior to the coming new age, should be used not only to support the concept of the New Age about to arrive, but should also feed those Christians who long to find evidence that the antichrist is coming, and who see the New Age Movement as fulfilling this hope. They are very much two sides of the same coin.

The New Age Postponed

The New Age concept received a mighty blow when the Roman Empire converted to Christianity during the fourth century. While there were millions of Christians outside the Roman Empire, those within it now faced a society in which the secular and religious were intertwined. This meant that visions of the State becoming the all-powerful antichrist force foreseen by both Daniel and Revelation were no longer possible. At one level, the State had been made Holy - as was explicitly stated in the later mediaeval concept of the Holy Roman Empire. At another level, the Church no longer hoped for the new age because it had become established and had inaugurated its own new age of Church-State relationships. It thus fell to the 'heretics' to continue the hopes for a new age when the corruption of the present age would fall away and the new age of the spirit would come. For centuries, various ideas about a new interpretation of history and of a new age played around the edges of Christianity in the West; it is important to note that no such ideas played any significant role in the thinking of the Eastern Churches such as the Nestorians or the Syrian Orthodox Church in India. But while these ideas remained on the edges of Christianity, they failed for a long time to make any really deep impact on mainstream Christian thought. This was to come, almost by accident, through the writings and teachings of a very orthodox monk and hermit of the twelfth century.

The Three Ages Model

In the twelfth century, a Calabrian abbot and mystic proclaimed that he understood the forces of history and the way of the future. Joachim of Fiore (1145-1202) had engaged in that most dangerous of occupations, decoding the Books of Daniel and Revelation. His researches, combined with a revelation, gave him to interpret the message thus. He saw history moving or evolving through three successive and ascending eras or phases. These stages moved from a primitive to a perfected condition. The first stage or Age was that of the Father. This was the time of the powerfully jealous God of the Old Testament, who laid down laws, because people were so primitive that they needed controlling through fear and authority. This Age had lasted from Abraham until immediately before the birth of Christ and had been being born from the time of Adam until the time of Abraham.

The second Age was the Age of the Son or the Gospel, during which people lived by faith and by submission as sons of God to the Father. This Age had begun to emerge in the time of the prophet Elijah, finally coming into existence at the time of Christ who came to reveal this new Age.

The third and final Age would be the Age of the Spirit. In this New Age people would dwell without fear and without any need to submit, for they would live by love, with joy and in complete freedom. All society would be like one great community - Joachim saw it as a vast monastery of equals all living in perfect bliss and blessedness with each other and with nature. He believed that this new Age had been coming into existence since the time of St Benedict (480?-543) and that by the year 1260 this new Age of the Spirit would have arrived in its full splendour. For Joachim, the start of the thirteenth century was the start of the realization of the new Age and it was this exciting message which attracted so many people to take up his teachings.

Needless to say, this new Age did not actually materialize, but the model proved very popular and in a remarkably short period of time Joachim's ideas had permeated widely throughout Christendom and were being updated or elaborated as first the decades and then the centuries rolled on with no sign or sight of this Third Age. The ideas deeply influenced Europe and excited those who wished to see a change or reform of Europe. Joachim's prophecies are one of the contributory factors behind both the Renaissance and the Reformation.

The Recurring New Age

At times of serious social, economic and cultural dislocation, religion and religious movements arise with utterly predictable regularity. As Norman Cohn has shown in his splendid study of messianic movements and social tension in Europe from AD 1000 to the sixteenth century, *The Pursuit of the Millennium*,[1] many of the dimensions of the contemporary New Age movement could be found functioning in the overcrowded cities of the Netherlands in the twelfth century, amongst the displaced peasants of the Rhine in the thirteenth century or arising in the independent and volatile city states of Italy in the fourteenth and fifteenth centuries.

In his studies of the roots of and consequences of the English Civil War of the mid-seventeenth century, Christopher Hill has shown how utopian, apocalyptic and communardist groups emerged from the chaos and social upheaval of that most momentous period of English history. Messiahs, prophets, psychics and new society planners suddenly burst into sight – they had always been there, but now the times seemed most suited to their message and the power of both Church and State had been greatly weakened.

As a child I was deeply interested in such movements, many of which would today be called New Age. For instance, my own family city of Bristol was the scene of an extraordinary event. In 1656, a very dramatic, charismatic preacher prophet suddenly announced, through his most devout female disciples, that the Christ would return to earth and would ride into Bristol to inaugurate the Heavenly Kingdom. On 24 October, one James Nayler proclaimed that he was Jesus Christ 'reincarnated'. Seated upon a horse, Nayler rode into

Bristol along roads strewn with cloaks, flowers and other 'tokens of thanksgiving', while his followers sang hosannas and danced through the streets proclaiming the reincarnation of Christ in James Nayler and foretelling a heavenly kingdom which was to come upon earth as a result. Today he would be assumed to be a New Ager and no one other than the fundamentalists would worry much; as it was, the good burghers of Bristol arrested him and then branded him.

The point I am making is really a very simple one. There is nothing whatsoever extraordinary about new religious movements, groupings, prophets, messiahs and the such like, emerging at times of social stress; indeed, one ought perhaps to be worried if they did not appear. They are not in themselves, therefore, harbingers of a New World. Far from it. Often they are, in fact, retreats from the harsh realities and painful choices imposed by social, cultural and religious upheaval.

Any student of the great spiritual revivals of the eighteenth or nineteenth centuries will know that such movements always threw up alongside the great evangelists, some very odd characters who flourished in the hothouse atmosphere of such revivals, many of which would now be called New Age. Gnosticism, magic, the occult and numerous other aspects of contemporary spiritual searching have always been present and active during such epochs. So has the belief that we stand on the edge of a brand new world. The early Christians thought so and saw their entire world being turned upside down and transformed. The utopian groups throughout the Middle Ages believed that theirs was the time described in various prophetic books, wherein the new age would break, the old world fade away and all human society be radically changed. The utopian communities which

settled the Americas, and the revolutionary and pacifist
religious groups which emerged during the English Civil
War all believed that they were standing on the edge of the
new world, the new age which would transform all life, or
at the very least, which had transformed and was
transforming their lives and opening them to powers
never previously expected or experienced. It was Thomas
Paine who in 1776 in his pamphlet *Common Sense* wrote:
'We have it in our power to begin the world over again. A
situation, similar to the present, hath not happened since
the days of Noah until now. The birthday of a new world
is at hand.' What we got was the industrial revolution, the
French Revolution, American Revolution, the USA and
consumerism - but the vision was certainly an exciting
one!

The Utopian Prophecy

In many New Age writers of today, the model of the three
ages, of an evolution of human behaviour linked to
progressive revelations of divine wisdom and freedom,
can be found. Joachim has been described as having
unleashed a system of prophetic utopian thinking 'which
was to be the most influential one known to Europe until
the appearance of Marxism.'[2] One can go much further
than this and say that just as it was waning in Europe in
the seventeenth and early eighteenth centuries, it
transferred to North America where it has never ceased to
be the most powerful influence, given that Marxism never
took hold in the USA. Echoes of the belief that the New
World was the place where a New Society of equality and
justice could come to be influence American thinking of
today.

This idea of evolutionary history has influenced thinkers such as the German Idealist philosopher Gotthold Lessing (1729-81); the scientific philosopher Auguste Comte (1798-1857) in his model of the three stages of history, religious, metaphysical and then scientific; it is even present in the three stages of Marxism, primitive communism, the class society and finally real communism. Now it is expressed in such New Age writers as Dr José Argüelles and Riane Eisler. In radically different ways and for radically different reasons, Argüelles and Eisler have provided new ways of assessing the past and foretelling the possibilities of the future.

Both are deeply imbued with the three ages thinking of Joachim, though they draw on different models. Argüelles uses a defunct Mayan calendrical system to predict that we are now entering a new age, the age of Harmonic Convergence, when all will work together and inter-space beings will come to guide us. Eisler, in a far more important and serious study, sees us having moved from a 'gylanic' age in which men and women were equals, through an age dominated by patriarchy, and presents us with the possibility that we stand now on the edge of a new age in which, as she sees it, complete harmony will be regained:

. . . this gylanic world will be a world where the minds of children – both girls and boys – will no longer be fettered. It will be a world where limitation and fear will no longer be systematically taught us through myths about how inevitably evil and perverse we humans are. In this world, children will not be taught epics about men who are honoured for being violent, or fairy tales about children who are lost in frightening woods where women are malevolent witches. They will be taught new myths, epics and stories in which human beings are good; men are peaceful; and the power of creativity and love - symbolised by the sacred Chalice, the holy vessel of life - is the governing principle. For in this gylanic world, our drive for justice, equality and freedom, our thirst for knowledge and spiritual illumination, and our yearning for love and beauty will at last be freed. And after the bloody detour of androcratic history, both women and men will at last find out what being human can mean. [3]

Eisler's vision is a classic Western one of a new age, and reflects many of the traditional facets of Joachim's Age of the Spirit. I think that Eisler's book is one of the most important to emerge from the new thinking which is often gathered together under the title New Age, and I shall be looking at it in more detail in Chapter 6. My reason for quoting her here is to show how the vision of a new age has remained remarkably consistent down the ages. Indeed one could argue that it is a perennial way in which *Western* minds think. I stress Western minds because, despite the claims for universality within the New Age, it is almost entirely a Western-dominated development. Only Western Christianity developed this model of the new age; it was unknown to the Persian, Chinese and Indian churches of the Middle Ages. Likewise, whilst the New Age likes to play with titbits from Eastern religions such as Buddhism and Hinduism or Taoism, none of these faiths (with the exception of certain Japanese Buddhist groups) has this belief in a new age, an age of wisdom and of bliss. Indeed, quite the reverse. Both Hinduism and Buddhism teach that far from being on the verge of a new and improved world, a world which is evolving from the primitive to the sophisticated, we are actually degenerating and are entering the last and most debased era of this planet's current existence. Both Hinduism and Buddhism teach a cycle of birth, growth, decline, death and rebirth. This affects not just living creatures, but the planet as a whole and indeed the entire universe, for it is in the very nature of things to go through such phases. Currently, so most Hindu teachings say, we are well into the era of decline and degradation – the final period of time called the Kali-yuga – at the end of which human life will have sunk to an all-time low, resulting in the destruction of this planet and all life upon it. Millions of years later a new world and new species will arrive. As for Taoism, its interest is in perpetuating and sustaining a balanced relationship between Heaven, Humanity and the Earth, an aim which it believes it achieves through practice and liturgy. There is no New Age in Taoism but a search for ways to perpetuate the best of the past in the present in order to ensure there is a future.

So the notion of a better time, a new and glorious era about to break upon us if only we dare to hope and trust and work for it, is a very particular Western Judaeo-Christian notion. There is nothing new about it, nor is there anything universal about it. We need to be careful therefore in assuming that the notion is a sound one, no matter how inspiring it may seem. It is a very particular belief.

I want to turn now to the whole issue of the rise in religious and spiritual awareness and in particular, to the issue of our supposed innate human potential – the 'God within us' notion.

Fads, the Fringe and Faith

At any time of social, religious and cultural upheaval,

ideas, groups, movements and individuals who would normally not appear significant or attract attention, do so. The reasons for this are diverse: sometimes it is because the stranglehold of traditional guardians of orthodoxy has weakened and thus these ideas and movements can surface; at other times it is because a genuine spirit of enquiry is about and both the wise and the foolish, the mystic and the conman seek to respond to the new atmosphere of interest; occasionally it is because major changes in religious thinking are actually taking place and before a new orthodoxy can arise, variety becomes the flavour of the month or year and there contend 'a hundred schools', as the Chinese put it.

Again, there is absolutely nothing new about what we see being touted as New Age; it is instructive to look back in time and see what was being offered at earlier periods of religious and cultural change.

The time of Christ is one such period. The old religious beliefs of Rome had become little more than civic duties. Into the vacuum that was left and into the cosmopolitan mixture that was the hallmark of the great cities of the empire, came a vast array of religions, cults, beliefs and practices. Many of these came from the 'mysterious Orient', for even in those days anything from the East was considered more exotic than home-grown ideas. Mystery cults and death and resurrection religions such as those of Isis or Mithras were in great demand. Astrologers, fortune-tellers, mystics and magicians were all eagerly sought and patronized. When it came to beliefs about life and death, everything currently present in the mishmash of the New Age was present 2000 years ago in the interest in subjects such as reincarnation, resurrection and existence on another planet. In the backstreets of Rome, Ephesus or Alexandria, you could be initiated into any

number of societies, faiths and cults which would offer
you superhuman powers or immortality or sexual success
or influence over the forces of evil. In their market places
you could have your fortune told from the entrails of
animals, from your palm, your face or your birthday.
There were fads for owning meteorite stones – believed to
be deities in their own right – and for sacred numbers,
letters or amulets, which were believed to bestow powers
upon the wearer.

In other words, just about any of the dimensions of the
New Age-type, fringe religious practices which exist
today, you could have bought, entered into or observed at
the time of Christ. Nor did these all cease or go
underground when Christianity, some three hundred and
fifty to four hundred years later, became the official faith
of the Empire. It is perhaps important to stress that it was
only with the rise of the Renaissance and in particular the
rise of the Protestant tradition, with its strong anti-
papist/anti-superstition mentality, that Christianity took
a firm line against fortune-telling, horoscopes and the
such like. Marco Polo is most informative on this. In
describing the courts of the Khans through which he
travelled in the late thirteenth century, he tells of the
Christian fortune-tellers, astrologers and horoscope
readers he found there, alongside the Muslim, Buddhist
and shamanist practitioners of these arts. For Polo, there
was nothing strange in Christians engaging in such
activities; what was novel was that they did so beside
others from different faiths.

Another society which manifested a fascination with
the fringe aspects of religion was that which thrived in the
city states of Italy during the earliest periods of the
Renaissance. Here, in Venice, Florence or Genoa, a
quixotic mixture of analytical science, perspective art,

Greek and Arabic learning, magic, occult practices, corrupt Christianity and austere monasticism, self-improvement groups, mutual support communities, fortune-tellers, astrologer and other such folk, rubbed shoulders and sought meaning in lives which were increasingly complicated and fragmented by trade, warfare, a venal religious structure and widespread corruption and abuse.

A similar story can be told for other periods such as the English Civil War, the French Revolution and its aftermath, or the post-First World War era when the old orders were seen to have collapsed in the folly of the trenches and there emerged people like my grandfather, offering a means of making esoteric sense out of disorder and fragmentation; offering purpose and direction when all established signposts had fallen away.

So when certain Christians, and others, look askance at the sillier aspects of the current spiritual revival such as healing crystals, horoscopes, divination systems, esoteric teachings and the such like, they should be reminded that these have always been around and have always accompanied any religious upsurge - even Christian revivals. Furthermore, these fringe aspects have always fulfilled the same function, namely, to offer a sense of being in control, or of being in touch with the forces which ultimately are in control, of what is happening. Because religious revivals occur at times of social stress, it is only natural that they should manifest tendencies that seem to offer special skills, knowledge or insights, for through such means do people regain or feel that they have regained some degree of security and control over their lives and over the interpretation of the events unfolding around them.

Rebellion and the Religious Response

There are certain classic hallmarks of what constitutes a time of social, cultural and religious upheaval and of the religious and spiritual response to these issues. Firstly, older forms of authority collapse or are so severely challenged that something has to give. At the time of Jesus it was the collapse of the civic religion of Rome, which had offered nothing to the individual. At the time of the Renaissance and the Reformation, it was the collapse of the central authority of the Roman Catholic Church and the emergence of conflicting authority bases, national identity being one of the key ones. In England during the Civil War it was the attacks on the Established Church and the destruction of the monarchy with the beheading of Charles I. During the French Revolution, it was the eradication of the monarchy and the over-throwing of the entire order of France, from landlords to the Church. Following the First World War it was the dismantling of the old European empires, the rise of Communism and the apparent inability of institutional religion to respond to the changes. Today we have many of these self-same factors: in many countries which were traditionally called Christian, the churches have lost not just numbers but moral, ethical and spiritual ground, while government is seen as venal, or at the least self-serving, and authority *per se* is suspect.

The religio-spiritual response usually follows a predictable course. It may be an attempt to reform the existing religious structures, the Reformation being one such example. Alternatively it may be to offer a secure world view, which seems new and thus untainted by association with the fading religious structures; or which provides a view of the world which either excludes from consideration all else that is happening except the affairs and ideas of the religious group itself, or includes everything in a rosy view wherein the faithful see themselves as having a deeper and more spiritual understanding of the world. The basic function of religious and spiritual groups is indeed to construct world-views within which people can live and through which people can make sense of the world. That these become even more necessary at times of social, cultural and religious flux is self-evident. That many of these advocate world-views and means of interpretation that are ultimately irrelevant is a fact of religious life. But we should never be surprised that such a plethora of diverse and at times downright odd world views come into being at such times. That is how our psyche and our culture deals, at one level, with collapse, stress and change.

Within all this upheaval, it is interesting to observe the role and significance of the individual. Essentially, times of stress throw up two different models for the individual. The first is sublimation within a group or movement which 'has the truth' or 'knows where it is going', so that the individual becomes part of that group or movement and surrenders the anxieties of personal direction and the search for meaning to the greater authority and certainty of the group or movement. Certain forms of fundamentalist or charismatic Christianity, the Unification Church, Scientology, and National Socialism are all examples of such a sublimation model. The religious world of today is full of examples, ranging from fundamentalist Buddhist groups, millenarian Hindu societies and any number of 'Eastern' or Higher Master-dominated organizations. They all offer a sense of superior knowledge and certainty, security amidst the changes and fluxes of life and an authority by which all events and one's own place within them can be interpreted. They always describe themselves as either 'new', because this denotes their lack of any link with the existing power structures, or they present themselves as 'original', that is, as going back to the original teachings, long since 'distorted', of teachers such as Buddha or Jesus.

The second model is very different. This turns away from the security and authority of the group or teacher, towards the power and authority within the individual. It emphasizes a person's inner potential, which can be unleashed or linked up to some greater source or origin of power. In the past, such individual empowerment processes were described in conventional religious language. St Athanasius (c.296–373), for example, taught that through the Word, the Logos, God is united with humanity and makes it possible for the fallen image of God within humanity to be restored; the divine potential within each person can be realized. As Athanasius put it, 'God became man, in order that man could become God.' Now to many Christians, such a statement would sound like a typical New Age claim. Indeed, one of the major problems which the fairly pro-New Age theologian Ted Peters has in his study of the New Age, *The Cosmic Self*,[4] is with the claim that God can be within and that we all have the power to become God (see Chapter 3). Yet there is a strong mystical tradition, particularly within Orthodox Christianity, which has always claimed this. It is perhaps important to bring this to the fore and to look at what it means for Christianity. It has not only been expressed in Orthodoxy, but also in the Roman Catholic and, perhaps surprisingly, Methodist traditions.

God Within Us

Jean-Pierre de Caussade (1675-1751), a Frenchman, became a Jesuit and rose to be rector of some of the major French Jesuit colleges before retiring to be a spiritual director at a seminary. In his book of spiritual direction, *L'Abandon*, counted as one of the greatest spiritual guides ever written, he explores the achievement of perfection and of sanctity by total abandonment to the love and power of God: 'I wish to show all that they may lay claim, not to the same distinct favours, but to the same love, the same self-abandonment, the same God, the same work for him and consequently, all without distinction, to an eminent sanctity.'[5]

It is difficult to summarize de Caussade's thinking in a few sentences, but essentially he sees the abandonment of self to the love and power of God as meaning that God can fill the soul, and thus the soul - the person - can become part of God. This is not so much an innate God within, but an emptying of the illusions of self so that God can fill the vacuum and draw us into the perfection, sanctity and eternity of the divine. As de Caussade describes it, 'If we knew how to leave God's divine hand free to act, we should attain the most eminent perfection. All would attain it, for it is offered to all.' Unlike much New Age thinking about the god within, this is not a development of our own personal ego or self, but an emptying of the ego and a being filled by God in order to do the will of God and thus achieve perfection and sanctification.

In Methodism, a similar notion to those of St Athanasius and de Caussade was articulated by its founder, John Wesley (1703-91). What he taught has often been quietly ignored or reinterpreted by later Methodists who frankly could not accept what he was saying. In many ways, the spiritual revival generated or developed by Wesley was very similar to the New Age. Wesley is, indeed, a fascinating figure who was rejected by his own religious hierarchy.

The specific aspect of Wesley I want briefly to mention is his teaching of holiness, of 'Christian Perfection', or 'Entire Sanctification'. Again, the idea is that the Christian gives up his or her life to be filled by God and thus becomes a part of God, wholly holy, sanctified or perfect. Wesley saw this as being a long process of realization of the divine within oneself. It was not instant, but it was possible. Nor was this perfecting of the divine within purely a personal thing; for Wesley it was both personal and social. Perfection showed itself in love for the wider community - for if God dwells within, surely that person, the perfected one, would demonstrate just the love of neighbour shown by Christ.

Much of Christian and Jewish mysticism is concerned with this individual engagement with the God potential within us, or of our potential once we allow God within us. That it has not been commonly perceived as being part of the Christian tradition has to do with the constant emphasis on the remoteness and authority of God rather than on the indwelling nature of the idea of incarnation. Christianity, of all faiths, should be able to handle in a mature way the concept of both a God without and the divine within, or at least the potential for the human frame to contain and reflect the divine.

In our own age, few people have been aware that this tradition of the 'God within' is to be found in Orthodoxy, Catholicism, Methodism, and in fact is fundamental to Christian incarnational thought. Thus they have turned to other ways of expressing this insight, of the divine within responding to the divine beyond, a holism of which few Christians have been aware in their own faith. Furthermore, as conventional religious language has become increasingly irrelevant or tainted, people have turned away from it and have found new words for the same phenomena. Psychology, psychoanalysis, co-counselling, self-awareness courses and so on have provided a new vocabulary and set of symbols to express this age-old idea. Many Christians find that the words used about self-fulfilment, self-awareness and so forth sound alien, whereas in fact there is little new in any of these newly described ways of developing the individual and of thus finding a place and purpose within the greater order of things. The same essential human need for meaning and security is being addressed whether it is by St Athanasius or by a Californian human potential developer.

Human Potential and Happiness

There are dangers, however. The Christian understanding of someone such as Athanasius is always shaped and tempered by the knowledge of failure and of having to try again. After all, the supreme Christian expression of the divine within the human – Jesus Christ – is a story of moments of great ecstasy, betrayal, times of joy and of crucifixion. To realize the potential within may be a very disturbing experience and will certainly not fulfil that most glib of promises – happiness. The assumption that human potential development leads to peaceful, contented existence is without any evidence. The more one realizes what is possible, the more one is also taunted by the confines and realities of working within an

imperfect world in which others' visions of realizing their
potential may well be at your expense and vice versa.

This illusion of human potential bringing happiness is
not confined to the fringes of the New Age. It is also
present on the fringes of Christianity. I recall once
walking out in disgust from an evangelical concert in
Cambridge, England. The lead singer had just claimed
that if you trusted in Christ and called him into your life,
you would never suffer again, nor be unhappy, nor fail at
anything you wanted to do. To me, this seemed a terrible
falsehood, so much so that I left in great anger. Christ
never offered an easy life, and spirituality, true
spirituality, is a costly and painful process as any of the
mystics, East or West, will tell you if you read them. But
the desire to have easy and if possible instant
gratification, to overcome all the weaknesses and flaws
within us at one bound, and to be more capable, more in
control and more effective, is very deep seated, for the
simple reason that we are actually always falling short,
proved to be weak and failing to live up to what we think
we can do. There is nothing new in human potential
movements, except their use of language. Nor is there
anything new in people seeking to be greater, more
powerful or more in control that they have been - or in
people discovering how ephemeral most of the
techniques and promises of greater potential are. To
realize the God within may lead you to crucifixion as well
as to the mount of transfiguration. To assume it will
always lead you down the Yellow Brick Road to Happiness
is simply to exhibit immaturity.

Bedevilled by Dualism

Finally, in this religio-historical chapter, I want to look at the central role of dualism within both the New Age movement and within the response to it by certain Christians.

I have written extensively elsewhere about the extent to which dualism shapes our contemporary cultures in the West. [6] Here I just want to look at the way in which the New Age reflects the traditional divide in Western crisis response between Utopia and Apocalypse.

Our problems began back in the exile of the Jews in Babylon in the sixth century BC. Prior to this time, Judiasm did not have a dualistic outlook. It saw both good and evil as emanating from God, as Isaiah 45:7 makes clear:

I am the Lord and there is none else.
I form the light and create darkness;
I make peace and create evil;
I, the Lord, do all these things.

In exile in Babylon, in the chaos caused by the destruction of their Temple, their homeland and much of their way of life and beliefs, the Jews were very susceptible to new ideas about the force of evil, and were willing to look at new ways of interpreting history which gave some meaning to the trials and tribulations through which they were passing. In Babylon they encountered the dualistic thinking of Zoroastrianism, in which the great god Ahura Mazda, the force of good, was opposed by an equal force for evil called Angra Mainyu. Gradually, the Jews absorbed this model, so that in their later writings, they began to speak of a force if not actually equal to God, at least representing a power which contradicted God and from which all that was evil emanated: Satan or the devil. Traditionally, Satan had simply been God's prosecuting agent, as in the story of Job, and as he appears in the role of the tempter of Jesus, testing Jesus' understanding of his mission on behalf of God. At no point in the Jewish Bible – what Christians call the Old Testament – does a figure of evil working powerfully against God appear. The devil is not in the Old Testament and Satan is simply the lawyer for the prosecution. Over time, and especially at times of mass persecution – such as under the Seleucids in the mid-second century BC or under the Romans as in AD 66–70 – the Jews developed their own dualistic world-view, one which the Christians, or rather some Christians, also took up. In this world-view, there are two forces, good and evil. The world is held in thrall to evil and it requires the breaking in of good, or God, to break the hold of evil. The world is thus seen, as is history, as a battleground between these two forces. At times of social change and stress, this tension between good and evil is seen to be even more intense. Groups that have felt themselves to be on the edge of a new age have always portrayed the choice before us as being between the evil of the past and the good of the potential future. They have presented a sort of Hobson's choice: do you want to go on living a life which is, say, morally corrupt, destroying the planet, or patriarchal and oppressive, or do you want to live in happiness, peace and equality for ever? This is the sort of romantic vision presented by writers such as Eisler (see page 37).

I would contend that life is actually not that simple, and in fairness Eisler is also aware of life's complexities, as we shall see later. However, the dichotomy of good and evil means that we have inherited a tendency to see the world in simplistic, black and white terms, an inheritance reflected in most New Age pronouncements about the state of our existing culture and the potential culture or world which is about to break in upon us, if only we would let it. It is also present in many political statements, such as Ronald Reagan's contention that the old Soviet Union was the 'Evil Empire', or the allies' naive declaration that a New World Order had been created after the defeat of Iraq in Kuwait. The collapse of these particular myths has been spectacular and bloody - yet the rhetoric continues. To me, dualism is an at the least unhelpful, at most highly destructive side road in religious thought and belief and it does no justice to the actual complexity and greyness of much of the moral and ethical, political and economic, spiritual and religious choices we have to make.

Diversity, Unity and the One

The influence of dualism is unfortunately further compounded by the urge for the 'One'. Western religious, philosophical and political thought is dominated by the quest for a return to an absolute Oneness or Origin and for the ultimate sublimation of difference into the Same. The Hebrew tradition saw a place for diversity and the psalms often talk of God amongst the gods or in the Courts of Heaven as the chief amongst the others. But for the Greeks of Plato's time onwards God had to be absolute, remote and One - there could be no diversity in the ultimate nature of existence - and subsequently the West has found diversity threatening and frightening, because it has valued the idea of the One and in particular of the 'One Mind' above all else.

Plato (*c.*427-*c.*347 BC) was the first really to express the idea of the unemotional, unchangeable One. This was in contradistinction to the mass of fickle gods and superheroes with which Greek society was filled. To Plato, these were distractions and perversions of the truth that there is only One source of Being, and this One is beyond all emotion (does not get jealous); beyond all cajoling (does not take sides in wars); and is ultimately Good (though this is more developed by later thinkers) and thus beyond enmity. In a phrase which has had profound consequences for our intellectual development, Plato described this as Mind. In positing this model of the One, Plato was also opposed to any idea of dualism and to the idea that there was a struggle for power going on in the world. For him, such thinking would suggest feelings and commitment in the One, and this he was at pains to exclude, quite apart from the horror he would have felt at the idea that the One was in fact two.

The Greek concept of the One fused in the early centuries of Christianity with key texts within the Bible. These texts were often, in their true nature, totally at variance with the unmovable, unemotional One of Plato. The God of the Old Testament is an emotional God who cares for his chosen people and for creation in a dramatic and passionate way. It is the complete reverse of the cold, distant, unemotional One of Plato and his followers. For instance, it is unimaginable that Plato's One could have uttered words such as those from Hosea 11:1-9:

When Israel was a child I loved him,
and I called my son out of Egypt.
But the more I called to them, the further they went
    from me;
they have offered sacrifice to the Baals
and set their offerings smoking before the idols.
I myself taught Ephraim to walk,
I took them in my arms;

yet they have not understood that I was the one looking
  after them.
I led them with reins of kindness,
with leading-strings of love.
I was like someone who lifts an infant close against his
  cheek;
stooping down to him I give him his food.
They will have to go back to Egypt,
Assyria must be their king,
because they have refused to return to me.
The sword will rage through their towns,
wiping out their children,
glutting itself inside their fortresses.
My people are diseased through their disloyalty;
they call on Baal,
but he does not cure them.
Ephraim, how could I part with you?
Israel, how could I give you up?
How could I treat you like Admah,
or deal with you like Zeboim?
My heart recoils from it,
my whole being trembles at the thought.
I will not give rein to my fierce anger,
I will not destroy Ephraim again,
for I am God, not man:
I am the Holy One in your midst
and have no wish to destroy.

Likewise, the God of the New Testament is an emotional
one, who 'so loved creation that he sent his only Son' (John
3:16) and who is described by Christ as being like a mother
hen, wishing to gather all her children to her and to
protect them (Luke 13:34). Furthermore, as modern
theologies such as Liberation Theology or Feminist

Theology are showing in their telling of the biblical story, God has always had a preference for, a bias towards, the poor and the oppressed - a bias that was carefully ignored or explained away in spiritual terms for many centuries, not least because it did not fit the Platonic One model.

This Greek philosophical tradition profoundly influenced early Christianity during its first four or five hundred years of formation. Thus Christianity and its partial offsprings, Islam and then Marxism, all sought to impose one model of reality, one God or one system upon the diversity of the world. Again I must make the point that much of Eastern Christianity did not go down this path. But in the West, unity and uniformity became of the essence. This desire to make everyone do what you do, believe what you believe and form the same sort of society you have, continues to this day. Marxism, socialism, capitalism, consumerism, green politics - all these manifest the desire to make the world conform. If only everyone did as we do, believed what we believe, then all would be well.

This desire of the One, fused with the dualism of fearing diversity as being of the Evil One, is often powerfully represented in much New Age thinking. This age is portrayed as being evil, corrupt and dangerous. The future, on the other hand, is portrayed as being glorious, for if only people would stop doing what they are doing now - being in the hands of the evil one, patriarchy, old ways of thinking, you name it - and start doing what the New Age group think is good, then all would be well and we would return to the One, being one happy family. If we don't take their path, then we face destruction at the hands of these forces of evil. This very closely mirrors thinking to be found in millenarian Christian groups - those who believe that this Age is the most wicked, furthest away from God and most sinful - yet such Christians also believe that Christ is on the point of returning to earth and will rid the planet of all evil and suffering. Then will begin Christ's thousand-year reign (hence the term millenarian), which will be a time of unparalleled bliss and happiness. This strand of thinking has surfaced repeatedly at times of social strain in the West, and the New Age variety is almost identical to the more familiar albeit orthodox Christian approach. It is a game that has been going on since at least the time of Christ and, frankly, I believe we need to break free of this apocalypse-utopia dichotomy and of this naivity concerning the nature of difference and unity. One thing that the New Age is actually not good at handling is diversity (see page 127 and Chapter 6), other than in a sort of live and let live mentality; when pushed, much of what calls itself New Age is in fact the old dualist/One argument simply restated.

So I would contend that there is nothing happening today in this so called New Age movement which has not been going on for centuries or even millennia. The New Age is simply the most recent expression of the tensions, hopes, dreams, opportunism and visions which arise at any time of social and cultural stress. Furthermore, far from breaking free from traditional world views, most of the material being presented, groups being formed and solutions being offered are nothing more than old models, well tried and failed, repackaged in modern language. The fear which the New Age inspires in some is largely a result of the fact that in past centuries such revivals, including the odd and peculiar, have used conventional Christian language. Even when what they did was unconventional, it at least sounded familiar. Now the language is more varied and eclectic, although I would contend that in essence there is nothing new - or at least, very little that is *really* new. In Chapters 5 and 6 I want to look at what I do believe is stimulating and potentially new in the New Age movement. But at heart, the very concept of a new age is millennia-old and arises naturally with just about every generation.

Chapter 3

Christ, The Antichrist and All Things New

In Chapters 1 and 2 I have argued that the New Age does not exist in the way in which so many of its proponents claim. What does exist is what has always existed: a search for new ways of living and understanding. In this field there are, as I will explore later, some fascinating new ideas being mooted, or rather new ways of interpreting reality, but new modes of interpretation have always been put forward. That they have little if anything to do with Tarot readers, crystal gazers or numerologists such as my grandfather I would also contend. Few if any of these practices are about new models of reality; most are used for such individualistic and ego-centred gratification that they often hinder intellectual exploration. That they are often seen as being a major bulwark of the New Age illustrates the extent to which the term is rendered almost meaningless. These practices have always been around, often in a somewhat parasitical relationship to whatever was the dominant religious or spiritual group or belief of the time. The hype about a massive movement of people seeking new paradigms is, perhaps sadly, a projection of certain people's beliefs and there is little evidence to support it. At one level, however, the hype of the New Age packagers has found converts, people who want to believe in the widespread hold and power of the New Age for one simple reason: they believe it is a sign of the coming of the Antichrist.

The New Age Conspiracy

Conspiracy theories bedevil Western society. Marilyn Ferguson plays clever games with the term. In her opening chapter called 'The Conspiracy', she paints a very romantic picture of tens of thousands of people working away to undermine the way society is today. While acknowledging that they are not organized into one group or set of groups and whilst also admitting that they are there for all sorts of different reasons, she still uses the term conspiracy to give the impression that all these people are working towards one goal or from one understanding. As such she presents an image of a network of conspirators quietly subverting the structures of society.[1] As we shall see in the next chapter, this is not new either and indeed, as was argued in Chapter 1, the very many different people and groups who are working for change differ as greatly in their visions and purposes as is imaginable. Thus to claim any conspiracy - in the singular - is an illusion, but a comfortable illusion for those who don't actually look at the range of groups seeking to transform society: Marxists, radical conservatives, Muslim 'extremists', Christian fundamentalists, Hindu fundamentalists, radical scientists and so forth.

While the idea of a single conspiracy is simply silly, it has been taken up with glee by those in society who want *a* conspiracy to fit into their particular ideas about the way the world will go. I refer to those from the right of the Christian world, some fundamentalists, others defenders of what they wish to call 'Christian values'. I want to look at the way in which these people need to believe in a New Age Movement – the capitals are intentional – so that they can have something to oppose.

The Fundamentalist Christian Response

As a Christian I am alarmed at the speed with which a veritable witch hunt has started up within the churches. While I shall be quoting mostly from extremist material emanating from the USA and from certain circles in the UK and Germany, I find that fear or 'caution' about the New Age has spread into what I would consider the more mainstream sections of the Church. Thus a diocese close to my home city of Manchester has appointed a New Age adviser to help the Anglican Church combat rising New Age ideas and notions. What is even worse is that the term New Age has now become a way of discrediting something before you have even bothered to look at it. This reflects an anti-intellectual attitude which ironically finds its counterpart in much of the anti-intellectualism of many who claim to be New Age. It is an attitude that implies a rejection of serious study, criticism or analysis in favour of emotive, highly subjective responses which frequently rely upon acceptance of a set of assumptions or beliefs which are not felt to be open for examination, but are there simply to be accepted. What became more and more clear as I read and discussed with people on both sides was that they mirror each other, and it could be argued that they need each other to give some validity and substance to their fantasies. In all of this, the really interesting ideas that are emerging about history, sexuality, God, spirituality, ecology and so forth, get brushed aside or are lost in the midst of trivia and sometimes nonsense.

So what is being said by the other side, the fundamentalists and others of their ilk, about the New Age? Just as I found much of what purports to be New Age trivial, boring, anti-intellectual and irrelevant, so I found much of the Christian reaction puerile, obsessive, silly and at times profoundly sick. As a Christian I can honestly say that virtually everything that those who attack the New Age claim about what Christianity means I would deny; most of what they seek to defend I would discard; and many of the issues that they see as central I would see as peripheral. At the end of this book I hope to set out what I understand to be the role and meaning of Christianity today, so with this disclaimer, let me introduce you to the conspiracy mentality of certain Christians, for it gives us an insight into the fears and fantasies of certain sections of both Christianity and of Western society.

Fear and Fanaticism

The cover of Caryl Matrisciana's book *Gods of the New Age* puts it succinctly. Emblazoned across the top are the words 'There is an unparalleled mystical conspiracy threatening today's world'. Likewise, Constance Cumbey's book *The Hidden Dangers of the Rainbow* makes its position clear with the subtitle stamped across its cover, 'The New Age Movement and our coming Age of Barbarism'. Or turn to Roy Livesey's book *Understanding the New Age* where we are informed on the cover that New Age activities are, in fact, 'Preparations for Antichrist's One World Government'. You are left in little doubt that these writers and their like are convinced that an organized, systematic plot exists to subvert 'Christian values' and impose an 'Eastern' culture. In case we haven't got the point yet, Constance Cumbey's book - which is as important on the opposition side as is Ferguson's on the New Age side - has a page given over to this statement as soon as you open it:

It is the contention of this writer that for the first time in history there is a viable movement - the New Age Movement - that truly meets all the scriptural requirements for the antichrist and the political movement that will bring him on the world scene.

It is further the position of the writer that this most likely is the great apostasy or 'falling away' spoken of by the Apostle Paul and that the antichrist's appearance could be a very real event in our immediate future.

It is vitally important to Cumbey's hypothesis that there be a plot, a single scheme which is being worked out by agents all over the world. For without such a plot, such a scheme, her contention that this is working for the antichrist falls down. She builds a case by use of exaggeration and innuendo. She also sets out a supposedly clear list of both the teachings and controllers of this Movement, who are credited with exceptional organizational powers and success. Cumbey takes as her starting point the eccentric advertisements placed in newspapers such as the *New York Times, San Francisco Chronicle, The Times* of London and the *Guardian* by Benjamin Creme in 1982. In these advertisements he

announced that 'The Christ' had returned, also known as
Maitreya, the Fifth Buddha, the Iman Mahdi, Krishna and
so forth. Creme, rather rashly as it turned out, claimed
that within a few months the Christ would reveal himself
by speaking telepathically to everyone on the earth at the
same time. Then a new world would be built. Again, we
need to note that this idea is nothing new, witness James
Nayler in Bristol (see pages 34-5), and illustrates the
whole millenarian strand in Western social religious
thought.

These rather sad advertisements have sunk into
oblivion in most people's memories. In none of the
guides, reference books or collections of New Age
writings or groups do you find any mention of Creme or
his ideas. At meetings I have attended, no one has made
any reference to him. Most of us have enough respect for
the oddball and the dreamer to allow them their
moments of splendour and then to allow them to sink
back into obscurity. But not Constance Cumbey. For her
these advertisements were 'the culmination of over 100
years of meticulous planning and labor by those seeking
this "Age of Aquarius". They have garnered the support of
some of the most powerful and influential individuals in
the world.'[2]

Cumbey is convinced that Creme represents just the
tip of a vast occult empire beavering away taking over the
world. Not only this, but she also actually believes
Creme! She believes that the Maitreya is here:

Who is Lord Maitreya? Is he the antichrist? Is he
already in the world today? Is he an ordinary man who
is demonically possessed?
Only the insiders of the New Age Movement
hierarchy know his true identity.

Maitreya is living somewhere. He eats. He sleeps. He paces the floor. He studies world conditions. He knows his time is soon.[3]

How extraordinary that the only people who seem to believe Creme's claims are those most opposed to him. But it is all part of the buildup that Cumbey wishes to develop and which has its denouement in her thesis that this is all part of a centrally manipulated takeover bid for the world:

Maitreya's followers are now in the last stage of the New Age scheme to take the world for Lucifer . . . What is the Plan?
     It includes the installation of a New World 'Messiah', the implementation of a new world government and new world religion under Maitreya.
     They have numerous political, social and economic goals, including the following:

- A universal credit card system.
- A world food authority which would control the world's food supply.
- A universal tax.
- A universal draft.

But there is more to The Plan - they intend to utterly root out people who believe in the Bible and worship God and to completely stamp out Christianity . . . .
The Movement is working quickly and efficiently to execute its scheme to take control of the world for Maitreya.[4]

Cumbey offers no evidence for these claims, in particular her claims of the design to root out Christianity. What she is doing is an old trick to be used when you attack perceived enemies: namely, you make them out to be programmed, ruthless and intent upon your destruction. Cumbey offers no supporting documentary evidence of these claims other than quoting from the sad ramblings of Creme. Instead she turns to that most dangerous of books in the Bible, the Book of Revelation, and claims that she can see the prophecies of the Revelation being fulfilled by the New Age Movement. In other words, she offers no objective information, but simply seeks to present a case for biblical fulfilment, and even here I feel she stretches the credibility of her readers to breaking point. Witness the 'logic' of her discussion of Revelation 13:13-15 as a vital text. The text says:

And he doeth wonders, so that he maketh fire come down from heaven on the earth in the sight of men, and deceiveth them that dwell on the earth by the means of the miracles which he had power to do in the sight of the beast; saying to them that dwell on the earth, that they should make an image to the beast, which had the wound by the sword and did live. And he had power to give life unto the image of the beast, that the image of the beast should both speak, and cause that as many as would not worship the image of the beast should be killed.

How does Cumbey link this to the New Age Movement (to use her capitalization)? Her approach is very simple. She concludes that the image talked about in this text is a hologram created in space by the use of laser beams. She then cites that laser projectors have been mounted on the top of the Cathedral of St John the Divine in New York City. She thus concludes that New Agers will use these projectors to create images of the beast in the skies and thus they will fulfil Revelation 13:13-15.

It is perhaps important to pause a moment here amongst these sad rantings and remember that Cumbey's book outsells Ferguson's *The Aquarian Conspiracy*, that videos based upon the book sell worldwide and that she is quoted with approval by many opponents of the New Age. Extraordinary as much of her argument seems to many, it is also widely believed.

After these opening sallies and tasters, Cumbey introduces the reader to her version of where this vast conspiracy comes from. She starts with the Theosophists founded by Madame Blavatsky in 1875. Here she sees the origins of an avowedly anti-Christian society setting out for world domination.

The Theosophists have indeed always had an antipathy to Christianity, for their views arose within an India which was being dominated and exploited by the West and by Christianity. But their mixture of bits of Buddhism, Hinduism and fantasies about Tibet have failed to impress more than a handful of devout followers over the last century and a quarter. Their attempt to establish a new Messiah in the shape of the young boy Krishnamurti, whom the Theosophists brought from India to England in 1910, collapsed about their ears when Krishnamurti rejected their claims in 1929 and pronounced a plague on all formal religion. I have rarely met a Theosophist who was not an old age pensioner and their branches and offices around the world have been closing faster even than Christian Science Reading Rooms or Methodist Chapels. To Cumbey, however, they represent an international body intent upon controlling the world - an intent in which she believes they have nearly succeeded.

From the Theosophists, Cumbey takes us to the next plank in her world conspiracy theory. Here for once she does actually cite someone who has had and continues to have an impact upon New Age ideas: Alice Ann Bailey (1880-1949). A fascinating woman in her own right, Alice Bailey was originally a Christian and even married an Episcopalian clergyman. She became involved with the Theosophists at the turn of the century and became a channel for one of the Masters, from whom the Theosophists claimed that they received their teachings.

Bailey soon began to develop her own teachings, which were much less idiosyncratic and eclectic than those of the Theosophists, but still marked by the traits of universalism and a basic belief that all the great religious teachers were avatars of the unknowable God. In Bailey's works there is a setting forth of a new world order and a call for a new world religion. On that score alone, Cumbey is right to point to Bailey as a formative influence on the mishmash of ideas of the New Age. Cumbey is also interesting in pointing out how very 1930s Bailey's ideas are and how influenced by anti-semitic and even quasi-fascistic notions are her plans for a new world order. But then Bailey was very much a child of the turmoil resulting from the collapse of the old imperialist structures and the birthpangs of what she saw as being a brave new world. Her work is interesting in that it shows how very different are the current notions of the way the world should go from those of the 1930s.

My impression is that Bailey's works are cited by many simply because she first set out the idea of a New Age and of changing minds and paradigms. Few plough their way through all her writings, though the Lucis Trust, founded by her in the 1920s, still promotes her ideas quite vigorously. However, it also provides a platform for many

other groups, ideas and ways of thinking. Far from being a
key plank in a world conspiracy, it offers a genuine place for
the exploration of ideas and beliefs. I was asked recently to
speak at their UK annual meeting and to give the key
lecture. I did so as a Christian talking about how different
religions understand the environment in radically
different ways, and the debate afterwards was very
vigorous and stimulating. While I would not agree with
everything the Lucis Trust says or promotes, I'm not
expected to either. But Cumbey would have us believe that
these writings of Bailey, and her foundations such as the
Lucis Trust with their now rather antiquated ideas of
Aryanism and control, Master and Teachers, have been the
blueprint followed religiously by the New Age Movement.
Even more than this, she insists that the plan set out by
Bailey is now nearing completion and is being ruthlessly
pursued. This leads Cumbey then to make the extraordinary claim that 'the program of the New Age Movement has complete identity with the programs of Hitler'.[5]

Bailey's writings are interesting, expressing as they do
the anxieties and hopes that so obsessed the 1930s. The
expressed need for a strong ruler and an overall authority
makes Bailey sound very old-fashioned today. The sexism
of her writings and the hierarchical nature of her beliefs,
coupled with some strands of Aryanism picked up from
Nazi thought, indicate that she was caught up in the early
approval for National Socialism which many people,
religious and otherwise, felt in the last few years of the
1920s and the first few years of the 1930s. In a world of
chaos, meaninglessness and the growth of 'godless
communism', the imposition of order and a strong,
spiritual and moral leader was what many people wanted;
a not dissimilar phenomenon can be seen today amongst
some sectors of society. Bailey reflects all of this and it is

for this reason that her message is not really one that many people who identify themselves as New Agers can take seriously. Her hierarchical vision is well captured in her Great Invocation. To a certain degree it expresses what St Paul believed when he wrote that he longed for Jesus to return so that the world could be put to rights. This of course did not happen and the Church grew to have a deeper understanding of how God works in our lives and shapes our future. But the Great Invocation is part of a long line of similar prayers from those who despair of the present order of things:

From the point of Light
    within the Mind of God
Let the light stream forth into
    the minds of men.
Let Light descend on Earth.

From the point of Love
    within the Heart of God
Let love stream forth into
    the hearts of men.
May Christ return to Earth.

From the centre where the
    Will of God is known
Let purpose guide the little
    wills of men -
The purpose which the
    Masters know and serve.

From the centre which we
    call the race of man
Let the Plan of Love and
    Light work out
And may it seal the door
    where evil dwells.

Let Light and Love and
  Power restore the Plan
  on Earth.

It is often comforting for people to believe that someone,
somewhere knows what is happening and is going to see
it come alright in the end. This is a fairly impoverished or
childish form of faith, but one which, ironically, both
Bailey and Cumbey and her like believe in. It is childish
religion, where Father or the Masters know best. Many
explorers in spirituality pass beyond this dependency
model, but it is a very comforting one for those who wish
to believe that the hierarchy knows best. But none of this
in the slightest way warrants the abusive comment of
Cumbey that Bailey's plan, the so-called blueprint of the
New Age Movement, is identical to the aims of Hitler.

Having thus provided her reading of how the New Age
Movement conspiracy was born and reared and having
convinced herself and no doubt many others that such a
conspiracy exists, she then proceeds to show how it fulfils
Prophecy. Taking favoured texts from the Bible, but
mostly from Daniel and Revelation, she 'proves' that the
prophecies are fulfilled by the New Age Movement and
the Creme Plan.

There then follows a chapter which, while going over
the top, does touch upon a fundamental concern about
certain writers and thinkers within the New Age world.
Namely, the anti-semitic and pro-Aryan sympathies of
some writers. Because of a particular understanding of
evolution (which we shall look at later), certain New Age
writers have taken over Social Darwinian ideas about the
black and oriental races being more primitive than the
white races. This is, as Cumbey rightly points out, a very
disturbing aspect of some otherwise very interesting

writers. I want to look at the incipient racism inherent
within much of the social evolutionary thinking which
so shapes New Age ideas, later.

But how, you might be asking, does Cumbey believe
that this Plan is being forced upon us? Well, she believes
that it is through infiltration of all agencies and
organizations and by recruiting individuals at places such
as health food stores and 'juice bars'! In saying this, she is
merely reflecting the grandiose claims of people like
Ferguson who would see anyone who tries an organic diet
or practises yoga before going to work in a government
office, as fully signed up members of a conspiracy. While
such claims are nonsensical, the idea that doing anything
or visiting anywhere which has slightly different ideas or
values from the mainstream culture is inherently
subversive has strong appeal. One of my colleagues, Liz,
a Christian and member of an evangelical church, was
recently discussing with a friend from her church the fact
that Liz's daughter had become a vegetarian. This
produced great concern in her friend who worried about
the fact that Liz would have to visit the local vegetarian
shop. When asked why this was a problem, the friend said
it was because New Age forces worked through such
shops.

This is yet another age-old tool in the conspiracy
theorist's bag. In times of great change, people are often
alarmed when old ways of behaving begin to change. They
are disturbed because they don't quite know what to
make of new ideas. Most people of course, simply find
that, over time, they have absorbed some of these new
ideas into their own way of life, but some resist, and it
becomes even more easier to resist if you can claim that
evil forces are at work in those aspects of contemporary
society that you find disturbing or challenging. This is

what Cumbey and her like play upon very successfully. It has even reached the stage where to be involved in ecology is seen as a sign of membership of the New Age – but more on that later.

Just as certain proponents of the New Age indiscriminately roll anything vaguely religious or spiritual into one bundle and claim it for their own, so those attacking the New Age do the same. Cumbey gives an example of this in her section that purports to show that the New Age is satanic. In the opening few paragraphs she argues that satanism lies behind the New Age: 'New Agers will often admit they are worshipping Sanat Kumara, Pan, Venus, Shiva, Buddha and other pagan deities. The name Buddha literally means "Lightbearer" – the same meaning as the name Lucifer.'[6]

This trick of 'showing' links which simply do not exist is unfortunately a trick of Christian fundamentalists as well as of many New Age writers. Here, Cumbey gives a very particular reading of the term Buddha – usually translated as 'enlightened one' – and makes it sound as if the Buddha is just another name for Satan. Nothing could be further from the truth, but in the strange world of such people, this does not matter.

We then come to one of the main planks in many fundamentalists' attacks on the New Age: namely, that it has managed to infiltrate the Church itself. This is, of course, the final denouement of any conspiracy theory. The enemy is within. The citadel has been breached. The response is also always the same: a witch-hunt starts. This is precisely the course pursued by Cumbey in her writings, and many of those who follow her adopt it in practice. Let Cumbey speak for herself:

Often clothed in seemingly Christian language, the

'spiritual' aspects of the New Age Movement have gained acceptance among the unsuspecting even within orthodox religious institutions. The Movement's political programs have also won widespread endorsement and advocacy among Christian denominations.

The New Age Movement is pushing for, among other things: global agencies to handle distribution of global resources, redistribution of the world's wealth, a new world religion, experiential religion (as opposed to religion based on scriptural authority and tradition), a universal tax, a universal draft, right-brain/whole-brain thinking (intuitive and subjective, as opposed to what they call 'left-brain' or analytical thinking), a teaching that all things are part of one whole, an emphasis on universal interdependence, and zero population growth.

All these concepts are beginning to rear their ugly heads in evangelical Christian books and publications. Some denominations have incorporated substantial portions or all of these points into their 'agenda for the 80's'.[7]

The fear of the outsiders being inside is an old one, one which Cumbey combines with the traditional pet hatreds amongst the fundamentalist and extreme Protestant wings, of the Roman Catholics and anything which smacks of a social gospel. Nor is it just those who fall outside her definition of what constitutes a 'true Christian' who come in for criticism. A particular target is the very influential evangelical writer, Ron Sider, whose books include *Rich Christians in an Age of Hunger*. This book has had a tremendous impact in awakening evangelical Christians to concern for the poor and powerless of the world. But to Cumbey, Sider is an agent of the New Age Movement and is doing his bit to further the satanic Plan of Bailey et al: 'The first thing noticeable about Sider's book to one versed in New Age lore is his use of a vocabulary prevalent among New Agers. Words such as Spaceship Earth, vanguard, holistic, New Age, and global village are a common part of his vocabulary.'[8]

Again, we have the fascinating yet also disturbing fact that Cumbey adopts the reverse approach to that of many New Age writers. They tend to take any movement of change and pronounce it New Age, despite the fact that most such movements have no origin within or substantial links with any specific New Age group or even way of thinking. Cumbey turns this tendency upside down by claiming that all such social gospel movements have been created by the New Age and are therefore satanic. It is interesting to note the extent to which these two groups mirror each other, removed in both cases from any sustainable reality.

Finally, Cumbey offers advice on how to save New Agers, many of whom, she contends, are involved because they are decent people wishing to help the world. But for Cumbey, there can be no help other than through Jesus Christ – not even, so one gathers, from those who follow Christ by helping the needy in the spirit of Matthew 25:31-46.

I have quoted at length from Cumbey's *The Hidden Dangers of the Rainbow* for two reasons. It was the first major book on the topic of the New Age to come from the right-wing Christian stable and as such it forms the basis for just about all the subsequent books by writers from that section of Christianity. The second reason is that due to her very clear style and her uncompromising way of putting things, she graphically illustrates the essential elements of the conspiracy theory: that the New Age Movement is satanic and is part of the preparations for the Antichrist.

I want to look quickly at some other fundamentalist or evangelical writers before turning to look at how the more mainstream churches and writers have reacted to New Age phenomena.

Conspirators and Catholics

While Cumbey is the leading anti-New Age writer of the USA, Roy Livesey is the principal anti-New Age writer in the UK. He and his wife publish the *New Age Bulletin*, which purports to monitor and track New Age infiltration worldwide. He has also written books such as *Understanding the New Age, More Understanding the New Age* and *Understanding Deception*. Livesey comes from the older school of conspiracy theory – the one that sees the dreaded hand of Rome in all that is evil. For Livesey, the New Age movement is as much a Roman Catholic plot as anything else and he sees the Vatican as one of the main sources for New Age ideas. Livesey also has a grounding in those old conspiracy theories whereby any social change or call for social change is suspect. Thus he assumes that anyone involved in revolutions is or was out to destroy Christianity and thus is an agent of some sinister plot. Take, for example, the way in which he manages to combine both his pet theories in one and a half paragraphs:

The Illuminati are no longer an openly acknowledged organisation but their satanically inspired philosophy remains a real threat. Lucifer is the 'Light', and the

Illuminati are the 'enlightened' ones. On May 1 1776 Adam Weishaupt launched his scheme for the destruction of all religion and existing governments. Amongst other groups it seems that this secret group described as the 'Illuminati' could still be important in organising the world's affairs, its geographical groupings, the world's economics and the drive to world government.

We shall see that Illuminism and the Illuminati may well have begun with Ignatius de Loyola, the founder of the Society of Jesus (the Jesuits) in the sixteenth century.[9]

Livesey sees the conspiracy in terms of an actual struggle for world domination through organizations such as the United Nations and even the World Wide Fund for Nature! Behind what he sees as the sinister global plans of such groups, he detects the hand of the 'Mystery Babylon, the Mother of Harlots described in Revelation 18', by which he means the Pope. Indeed, most of his first book, *Understanding the New Age*, is nothing much more than a reworking of classic antipapal Protestant rantings. In his second book, *More Understanding the New Age*, he does try to work in more from the New Age scene, following Cumbey very closely, and really takes off when he comes to the issue of the environment and the work which I and my colleagues undertake with the WWF on developing religiously based environmental programmes with eight faiths worldwide.

In 1986, the Duke of Edinburgh asked my group ICOREC (International Consultancy on Religion, Education and Culture) to organize on behalf of WWF International a gathering of major religious leaders at Assisi in Italy. Here we discussed the common concern for the environment found in radically different ways within the major faiths. We also launched a network to support the work undertaken by these religions, each in their own ways, for the care of the earth. This programme now has over 90,000 religious communities involved in environmental programmes ranging from reforesting the sacred forests of Krishna in India to developing environmental Sunday School schemes for all the mainline churches of Kenya. But to Livesey, the Assisi gathering has far more sinister implications. 'Looking over our shoulder do we see Rome again – in her familiar way, supporting movements that will serve her ends with a World religion based on Rome, and now encouraging the Earth Worshippers and animists, the ancient heroes of the New Agers?'[10] Needless to say the question is rhetorical and he answers it with a resounding 'Yes'.

Livesey is a much more conventional Christian conspiracy writer than Cumbey. For him, anything new is suspect and anything unfamiliar must come from Satan or Rome, or both. In *More Understanding the New Age* he provides a list of New Age occult forces. While many of them are the usual list of fortune-telling, ouija boards and horoscopes, the list includes some other, more surprising subjects. All of the following he describes as 'doors to the occult': Hallowe'en, Rudolf Steiner, fantasy role-playing games, judo, kung-fu, standing stones, tribal dancing, I Ching, Freud, 'holy' objects, Oriental ornaments, Stonehenge, demonized souvenirs, Buddhas, Indian elephants (I take it he means the little carved statues not the actual creatures!), pyramids and serpents.

Under the heading 'Cults' he puts, amongst many others, Baha'ism, Roman Catholicism, Communism, Islam, Hinduism, Buddhism and Zoroastrianism, while under the title 'Holistic Healing Therapies', which again

he considers occult, he includes acupuncture, moxibustion, reflexology, yoga, Bach Flower Remedies, herbal
concoctions, ginseng, the Alexander method, contemp-
lative prayer, psychotherapy, psychoanalysis and copper
bracelets.

However, in case this list alarms you, it is worth noting
that Livesey considers that the Narnia stories by the
Christian writer C.S. Lewis are also doors to the occult!

Again, I can only comment on the fact that both sides,
New Age and anti-New Age, play the same game. They
roll diverse and disparate groups, ideas and beliefs into
one ball and either claim it is all part of the New Age or
all part of the satanic conspiracy. Neither seems to pay
much attention to the actual beliefs and self-definitions
of the various groups whom they thus unceremoniously
bundle together.

As a Christian I am deeply saddened by much of what
I read coming from the right wing of the Christian faith.
It is a frightened faith: one which cannot handle the
changes in the world and which is fearful of anything and
anyone new. It is a sick faith for it seems to know nothing
of the love and openness of Jesus Christ nor of the ways
in which Christianity has always interacted with other
beliefs and systems. It is also a dualistic Christianity,
which believes that the devil exists and is a force equal to
God and that this world is, of its very material nature, a
bad place. These teachings, deriving as they do from
Zoroastrian dualism and gnostic teachings, are not part
and parcel of the original gospel of Christianity. In
promoting them, the fundamentalist Christians are
actually showing how they have lost sight of what the
Gospels tell us of Christ and Christ's ministry. Indeed, at
points, they advocate beliefs and ideas that would
normally be amongst those listed with approval by

certain New Age writers. It is this closeness that is so intriguing and that has some people wondering if the ever more frenetic style of certain churches, the use of hypnotic chanting and the singing of certain 'approved' types of music do not indeed represent a New Age version of evangelical Christianity!

There is plenty more of this oddball stuff; books that purport to show in ever more vivid detail what the New Age is doing. I think many evangelicals and fundamentalists buy this kind of material because secretly they are fascinated by the off-beat aspects of the New Age. If you believe in a real devil; in occult forces, in witches and in the idea that the Book of Revelation is a coded manual for the last days and that the Antichrist is with us now, then it is quite likely that you will also be fascinated by crystals, pyramids, fortune-telling, devil-worship and so forth. In other words, this obsession with the 'fringe' elements of religion is as much a feature of the fundamentalist and, in certain quarters, evangelical branches of Christianity as it is a feature of many who play with tarot cards or read their horoscopes. This is why the New Age so enrages its opponents, for they believe that people who are playing with these aspects of the New Age should be playing with their version of Christianity instead. The games are so similar that it is sibling rivalry, not fundamental opposition, that denotes the style and content of much that comes from the right of the Church in response to the perceived 'threat' of the New Age.

The New Age Doorway to the Gospel

There are, however, others writing from the Christian perspective who do not go quite down this line. Many evangelical writers, while still displaying this deep fascination with the oddball aspects of the New Age, see the New Age as being a very interesting and important statement about the revival of interest in religion and in spiritual issues. As I said at the start of Chapter 1, if, in the early 1960s, I had been catapulted forward into the late 1980s and 1990s, the thing which would have struck me most was the spread of interest in religion. The evangelical and fundamentalist churches have noted this and it distresses them that this spiritual revival, while very similar to earlier ones (see the previous chapter), is not leading people into the church or chapel. John Drane in his book *What is the New Age saying to the Church?* expresses well the nature of this concern:

Throughout the western world, the Church is losing ground and apparently has little to say to today's people. However uncomfortable it may be, we have to face up to the fact that people will not be brought to faith in Christ by what we are doing now. We no longer have the excuse that people today are secular and therefore not spiritually aware. They are more open to the spiritual than at any time this century.[11]

He goes on to ask why it is that when people need healing or community, they find it in alternative groups and not in the Church. He concludes that this is because the Church is not offering this to people. He sees the growth of interest in spiritual realities as very heartening:

Rapidly increasing numbers are finding it possible to believe in reincarnation, spirit guides and extra-terrestrials, and all sorts of esoteric ideas. To traditional Christians, this might be unfamiliar and threatening territory. But it certainly means that these people are spiritually open as no other generation within living memory has been.[12]

At one level Drane is saying, if they believe all that then they can believe our stories too; at another he is saying that, having had an interest in spiritual issues awakened, they can now tackle more substantial concepts and ideas – namely Christianity. Drane – in contradistinction to Livesey – sees interest in the occult or other forms of spirituality as a doorway to the Gospel.

The Archbishop of Canterbury, Dr Carey, while still bishop of Bath and Wells, was called upon to comment about the New Age. He was responding to a vicar in his diocese who had banned the WWF annual Christmas Carol Service on the grounds that because WWF worked with me on other religions and because other religions were satanic, I was therefore satanic and thus WWF was satanic. In the various newspaper articles that followed, the term New Age cropped up. In his diocesan newsletter Carey looked at the New Age phenomenon. He concluded that while he was not sure what it was, he felt that through the new wave of interest in the spiritual God was trying to tell the Church something. The Church, he said, should listen to what people found so helpful in New Age ideas and should then look within itself and see if the Church had anything to offer along those lines. The response of the Anglican Church in the UK has been very confused. Perhaps due to its own uncertainty about its role and identity it occasionally expresses 'concern' about the New Age, it has sections that condemn the New Age, yet it also has St James' Piccadilly, London, which offers a place for encounter with New Age ideas. This pattern is also to be found in most mainstream denominations in the USA, such as the Methodists.

A New Eightfold Path

Yet others see the New Age as opening up major new ways of understanding and they feel that Christianity can both learn from and contribute to these discussions. Typical of this approach is the book *The Cosmic Self* by Ted Peters. In a book that moves well from personal anecdote to theological or critical reflection, Peters responds very positively to many of the concepts that are coming out of the matrix we call the New Age. Like all of us he also enjoys telling of the quirky and the strange that he has encountered, but he takes seriously the intellectual challenges emerging from the New Age. In particular he asks us to engage critically with the new definitions of reality which modern science, psychoanalysis, feminist and ecological concerns are throwing up. Living as he does in Berkeley, California, he is right in the heartland of the New Age - what Ferguson sees as being the very centre of the coming new world. He detects eight major strands within New Age teaching, which he calls the Eightfold Path, a phrase to which some Buddhists would lay claim!

His eight 'basic tenets' are a very interesting tool for reflecting upon the elements of the New Age which can be discerned as having some sort of determining role. He starts with Holism - the belief that only by looking at something in its fullness or completeness can we understand it and any of its constituent parts. It is a reaction against the analytical nature of much of science, which examines the parts and is often felt to ignore the whole. Linked to this is his second tenet, monism. This is the belief that all things are part of one whole and that it is only by considering the cosmic whole that we can really know ourselves and the meaning of life. This ultimate whole is what New Age thinkers often refer to in conventional religious terms such as God, the Buddha or Vishnu, that is, the ultimate source is the total reality.

The third tenet is belief in The Higher Self; the idea that deep within us, beyond the conscious level, we are all united through being part of the whole. This unity is found at the level of the true self, a higher state of being than mere consciousness. The higher self is seen as a source of wisdom and healing, as an internal guide ready to draw us beyond our normal self. Some groups also claim that this higher self is in fact a divine spark which is trapped within the human body - a gnostic idea to which we shall return later.

Fourth in the Eightfold Path of Peters is Potentiality - or to be more precise, the Human Potential Movement. This teaches that we can all be more than we are currently, that the key to awakening this potential lies within us and that we have a right to do whatever it is that we feel we could or should do. We are presented with a vision of the human being as having the potential to do anything, to be a god in fact. Fifth comes reincarnation. I don't believe Peters is right in seeing this tenet as essentially an element introduced or promoted by the New Age. I think that reincarnation has always been a popular idea, even in the Christian West. It is at one level the most 'logical' solution to the problem of where do we come from and where do we go; furthermore, it is economical and a perfect example of recycling! On the housing estate in Manchester where I used to attend church, all the old ladies, committed, church-going, working-class women, believed in some form of reincarnation. In the early 1980s, research in the UK revealed that 80 per cent plus believed in God and 55 per cent believed in reincarnation. So, while I would agree reincarnation has become more openly discussed, I think it is a perennial question rather than a sign of the New Age.

Sixthly, comes Evolution and Transformation: the belief that we are evolving to be better, more advanced beings and that our age is the one in which humanity will take the next major leap forward in conceptual evolution and transform ourselves and our world. It used to be called Utopia.

Peters' seventh tenet is gnosis - knowledge. This is not knowledge as in scientific knowledge. It is true knowledge of the reality of the whole and as such it is seen as superior to scientific, quantifiable knowledge. Exponents of gnosis claim that we are largely moving within a world of darkness or, at best, of half-perceived shapes. Only through encountering the true knowledge can we break free of this shroud of darkness and see reality for what it is. This can be achieved, according to various New Age writers, through drugs, sex, spiritual training and so forth.

Finally, Peters has 'Jesus, sometimes'. This is an interesting point. He claims that Jesus is used in three different ways, one negative, two positive. The negative is as a symbol of the antignostic, Western rationalist world-view which is so opposed to the sorts of new visions the New Age claims as its own. It is the Jesus of formal Christianity, which is so often experienced as authoritarian, spiritually dead and obsessed with its own power and wealth. Positively, Jesus is used as a symbol of the human condition and our struggle to attain full potential and to move from the darkness of ignorance to

the light of gnosis; and as one of the teachers or Masters
so beloved of those sections of the New Age who want
hierarchies and Masters to tell them what to do.

Peters says that few if any New Age writers would lay
claim to all of these tenets, but he is right in seeing some
of them in all who claim to be New Age.

So where does all this leave a Christian writer and
thinker like Peters? In a position of what can be called
critical engagement. He is obviously challenged and
stimulated by some of what he encounters within the
New Age groups and individuals he has met. But he is also
alarmed by what he feels is the naiveté of much of the
movement, not least in the area of human development.
While he agrees that positive thinking is helpful, he
ultimately feels that unless this is balanced by a
recognition of the forces which shape us beyond our
control, by sin and by the actual reality of our own
situations, the New Age view 'will collapse under the
weight of its own naiveté'.[13]

Overall, Peters' book is a very sympathetic one in which
he tries to discern from the fruits of the New Age whether
any of it is of God. His conclusion is that much of it is. Yet,
en route, he turns to look at what Christianity has to offer
as a response to the issues that the New Age raises. Here
his particular background as a Lutheran comes out very
strongly. In essence, Peters simply presents those aspects
of traditional Lutheran theology that he feels need
restating in the light of the New Age, namely, Sin and
Grace; Justification and Faith; Sanctification and Love;
the Universal and the Particular. Much of what he has to
say under these headings is thoughtful and helpful, but I
cannot help feeling that in a sense his engagement with
some of the really stimulating ideas of the New Age has
left him essentially untouched. I believe that the

Protestant tradition of Christianity is in a much deeper crisis of meaning than Peters seems to believe. While this has little to do with the New Age as such, some thinkers and issues which are titled New Age present some fundamental challenges to the traditional language and even world-view of Western and especially Protestant Christianity. It is these challenges to which I want to return at the end of the book.

Peters concludes by offering four terse but very interesting reflections on the New Age. Remember, he lives in California, so sees the world through the eyes of the Californian romance with the New Age.

Firstly, he suggests, 'modest dabbling in new age spirituality is probably harmless; it may even be helpful'.[14] Many of the techniques which are now described as New Age are of course ancient spiritual methods of relaxation or meditation. But Peters also points to the development of newer techniques, such as psychotechnologies, and to the help these can give people following the insights afforded our generations by Freud and Jung amongst others.

Secondly, he points out that the 'new age vision is a noble and edifying one'. Many of the ideals that inspire the New Age vision of the future are found within the Christian vision of the coming of the Kingdom of God. The New Age vision is utopian, but many would argue it is an essential counterbalance to the destructive forces which currently dominate.

Thirdly, Peters urges that 'pastors, theologians, and church leaders should take the new age movement seriously'. He makes the same sort of point that Drane makes in his book, namely that 'new age spiritual practices are being sought because they appear to offer answers to urgent spiritual and political needs. This makes new age spirituality an issue of pastoral concern.'[15]

Finally, in his fourth point, Peters expresses his main worry about the New Age. For him, the major problem is 'the gnostic monism at the heart of new age teaching is dangerous because it leads to naiveté and to a denial of God's grace'. Indeed, Peters is so alarmed by this that he says, 'The intellectual stakes may turn out to rival those in the battle between Christianity and gnosticism, perhaps even the struggle between the Christian faith and paganism.' He comments that much of the New Age is callow and seems to have ignored the harsher realities of sin and evil. He can understand how appealing it is to believe 'that goodness and blessing and fulfilment are very close at hand – already within me – so that all I have to do is execute the right psychotechnique and I can bring it to full flower', but ultimately feels that this means an inability to handle the negative and destructive in our experience of life.

The Gnostic Influence

I believe Peters is overstating the case, because I would claim elements of gnosticism took control in early Christianity, in fact, and now need to be rejected for a healthier model. But he is also right about New Age naiveté. The view of gnosticism as more holistic than mainstream, 'rationalist' Christianity is very New Age. This is I believe one of its weakest planks, for gnosticism has been highly romanticized and is one of the major forces responsible for having created our present anti-environmental world-view. Gnosticism denies the validity of the material world, seeing it as the creation of a lesser force, even an evil force, meaning that the material world is in constant struggle with the higher, spiritual world. This attitude developed in the first three or four centuries AD in contradistinction to the emerging orthodox Christian understanding of creation as good and from and of God, yet it nevertheless managed to capture certain intellectual heights within Christianity through the conversion and writings of St Augustine. Augustine had belonged to a gnostic-type group, the Manichaeans. He was converted after ten years to Christianity, but he brought into his understanding of Christianity the anti-material, anti-sex and anti-world views of the gnostics. This in turn profoundly influenced the development of Western academic theology. It is this gnosticism that radical Christianity is rejecting in favour of pro-material world, pro-sexuality, pro-body theology.

However, gnosticism has become something of a fad within the New Age world for two reasons. It is seen as offering a form of Christianity which was suppressed and therefore must be valid; and it proposes a world-view in which those who are in the know are superior to those without the knowledge. In other words, most gnosticism appeals to the need for anything alternative to be rooted in our own culture and the desire to be superior which we all have to one degree or another.

The gnostic model of twin forces, good and evil, spiritual and material also offers a very simple method for evaluating all that one encounters. I believe that it is exactly this dualism which is one of the most serious obstacle to us understanding and reacting to the crises we now face, such as the environmental crisis. The significance of the gnostic influence on certain aspects of the New Age is that it is escapist in the extreme and shows the powerful hold dualism has over us, even when we think we are being new or revolutionary. It serves as a powerful reminder of how culturally conditioned we are.

Peters' is one of the most thoughtful, semi-positive books considering the Christian angle on the New Age. As such it comes as an immense relief and considerable stimulant following the rantings and fantasies of many other Christian writers such as Cumbey and Livesey. But I find he does not go far enough: while he is willing to allow that there is much good spirituality and the New Age quest, he ultimately feels the answer lies within a reiteration of basic, traditional Christian beliefs. I believe it lies in a rethinking and retelling of the Christian story and perhaps in the abandoning of certain kinds of Christian belief.

In conclusion, it seems to me that the majority of the Christian response to the New Age falls into two camps. The first is the 'they are the antichrist' approach; the second is the 'they are a manifestation of a spiritual quest, and we have the best answers'. At heart, what confuses many people from the churches is that in the past, spiritual renewals, revivals of interest in the religious, have been largely the province of the churches. Yet the history of periods of religious revival or of upsurge in religious interest has always been far more complex than most people have believed. In fact, the New Age is quite simply a traditional Western response to crisis and opportunity and yet again, there is little that is actually new about it.

Chapter 4

Just Because They Are Dead, Doesn't Mean They Are Right

In this chapter I want to look at what seems most to alarm some people about the New Age. This is not the new philosophies, the radically different models of reality, or the encounter between great traditions. No, what seems to dismay many people is what might be called the more fringe, peripheral and at times downright oddball activities which cluster under the umbrella of the New Age. I want however to consider such practices alongside some of the more cranky, sad and frankly sinister aspects of conventional religion. For yet again I would contend that there is little that is unique in the New Age fringe groups.

I think it is also important for me to spell out what my basic attitude is to much of the fringe, esoteric and silly stuff within both the New Age and conventional religion. To illustrate this, I want to tell a story about that great Quaker William Penn (1644–1718), founder of Pennsylvania. One day in Pennsylvania, a group of very excited Puritans brought an old woman before Penn in his role as magistrate. They accused her of being a witch. Penn replied by saying that there was no such thing as a witch.

The men insisted that there was and that furthermore, the woman had confessed to being a witch. Penn then asked the woman, 'Are you a witch?' 'Yes' replied the woman. 'Well in that case go in peace because there is no law against witches here', said Penn. But the men were not to be put off. 'But she flies through the air', they said. 'That is not possible' said Penn. 'But she does, we saw her' the men persisted, and the old woman echoed them saying 'I can fly, I can fly!' Whereupon Penn said, 'Well there is no law against flying in the state of Pennsylvania either!' and he dismissed them all.

I share this basic outlook. Many of the things people claim, I simply do not believe in nor do I consider them to be important. Having said this, unless they hurt people, abuse or exploit them, then why shouldn't people engage in harmless activities which give them some sense of power or purpose, peace or security?

The Medium and the Message

Let me start with one of the most popular aspects of the New Age, and one which while it has acquired a new name, has been around for centuries. That is channelling. The basic notion is that certain people act as a medium, a channel, through whom the dead communicate. In recent years, it has not just been the dead who communicate through such mediums, but also beings from other planets and realms of reality.

The method is normally the same. Namely, the medium goes into a trance-like state where they appear to be both asleep and yet also at the same time vibrantly alert. What happens next differs according to the individual concerned. Some mediums remain perfectly still while a voice, often quite unlike their own, speaks. Others will go into a state of high agitation and will then communicate. Yet others may use other means of communication such as writing down messages.

Such mediums and their messages have been recorded throughout history. In the Bible, the descriptions of the calling of many of the prophets and the accounts of how they received their messages make them sound very like contemporary channellers. One could argue that the claims of the prophets to be conveying a message direct from God is no more or less shocking than the claims of certain channellers today to be receiving messages from Jesus or from extraterrestrials. Perhaps one of the most graphic accounts of the prophet and his call and message is that of Ezekiel. In the first few chapters of his book are painted some very disturbing pictures of the ecstatic state and extraordinary actions which overtook Ezekiel. The dramatic nature of his call and commissioning has perhaps been dulled for many because this account is contained within the Bible. But looked at as a religious experience, it ranks amongst one of the most vivid and dramatic such experiences recorded.

The messages received by the prophets as we have them recorded in the Bible are profound and often very beautiful. They also spoke within a tradition which recognized the validity of such a message, and which had the critical faculties for assessing such claims. They bear little resemblance to the vast majority of messages received by mediums or channellers today, because they were concerned with the role of the Chosen People in God's salvationary plans for life on earth, with social justice, and with the place of the poor and oppressed in God's vision of human society, whereas most contemporary channellers seem concerned with individual issues and wishes for happiness. But we must not forget that these prophets of the Bible are but the very best, the most profound, and the most relevant of the many hundreds of prophets who lived and spoke in ancient Israel. We know that there was a whole class of priests known as prophets: the Bible talks about them going into trances, ecstasies or acting out messages, either individually or in groups. That only a tiny proportion of their outpourings came to be included in the Bible is obvious. Thus I suspect that, were we able to listen to what the vast majority of prophets had to say in ancient Israel, we would find it as banal and irrelevant as the vast majority of such material being poured out today.

One entire school of Taoism as a religious system is based on a revealed text which was given through two different mediums: this school is the famous Mao Shan sect of Taoism. Its origins lie with a remarkable woman, Wei Hua-ts'un (AD 251–334). She was a channel for various immortals within the Taoist tradition who gave her the first sections of the sacred texts of the Mao Shan school: the Shang Ch'ing scriptures. After her death, her school continued through her son and through a convert called Yang Hsi. In AD 364, Yang Hsi was summoned by spirits to a mountain top. Here, to his considerable astonishment, on Mount Mao, Kiangsu, Wei Hua-ts'un came to him from the dead and dictated the remainder of the scriptures. These scriptures are still revered and followed to this day.

Another example of channelling is the Qur'an. The story is a very familiar one of course, which is why we perhaps don't see it as the remarkable event that it was. Muhammad was a man in his early thirties who spent long hours in contemplation. Starting around AD 610, Muhammad began to receive revelation which he was ordered to write down. Over the years, the whole Qur'an was revealed to Muhammad and transcribed by him and his followers. The Qur'an claims to be a total and final revelation of the Word and Will of God for humanity.

In many societies around the world, the use of mediums to contact the dead or to receive messages is part of their culture. In Chinese Buddhism, monks who were gifted with mediumship would write on beds of sand answers or messages from the spirit world in response to questions from enquirers. Thus there is nothing particularly unusual in this art. However, in the West, we have had little experience of this, for the simple reason that Christianity, being a revealed religion, has seen itself as having received all that was necessary for human well-being. Indeed, it is interesting that mediums and the such like only began to appear in the last decade of the nineteenth century. It received a tremendous boost with the First World War. As millions of young lives were brutally and pointlessly snuffed out, as families lost father, sons and grandsons and the carnage built up, many sought to speak to those who had died so far away and for so little purpose at such a young age. Mothers, wives and lovers sought refuge with the spiritualists who seemed to make it possible for them and their loved ones to be reconnected.

At roughly the same time, people such as Madame Blavatsky were receiving teachings from esoteric sources such as her Tibetan and Hindu guides and Masters. The writings of Alice Bailey claim to have been revealed to her by beings such as a long-dead Tibetan Master, Djwhal Khul and a Master from another planet, Koot Hoomi. The very popular and Christian-based book *A Course in Miracles* is also claimed as a revealed text, and there are countless other examples.

Now, whether one considers there is anything of value in these revelations is an entirely personal decision. I find the prophets of Israel compelling and I find much within the Qur'an beautiful and moving and there are some insights within Bailey that are worth listening to, but Madame Blavatsky's writings speak not of eternity but of a very particular world-view which was only prevalent in the late nineteenth century. I find the Shang Ch'ing scriptures very interesting and respect the long tradition and use that the Mao Shan school of Taoism has made of them, while I find much of *A Course in Miracles* to be bland and self-satisfied. So I readily admit that I do not know quite what to make of these revealed messages which have come to form entire books, philosophies and ways of life. I suppose I remain largely agnostic, but not entirely. I have to acknowledge that religious history shows such messages to have been a fairly consistent phenomenon. But I also have to say that history reveals that tens of thousands of these messages have been reportedly received, and only a very few have ever survived long enough or been taken seriously enough to shape and affect religious life in any profound way.

Most of what is channelled is banal in the extreme and always has been. I recall sitting in on a seance in the late 1960s when Isaac Newton came through the medium. Here was one of the most interesting religious and scientific men of his age – and what did this great man want to say? He wanted to assure one of the women present that her husband would get better from his sickness. Today, you can talk to extraterrestrials who will reassure you that you will get that top job or increase your earning power, you can discuss sexual techniques with various Egyptian rulers or receive vague wisdom about being a better person from ancient sages from neolithic times. At other times, you can discover the particular interests of the medium. Thus, one Roman Catholic medium, Veronica Leuken in New York, channels the 'Lady of the Roses' - namely, the Virgin Mary. Leuken is a very conservative, that is to say right-wing Roman Catholic and her messages reflect this. Our Lady of the Roses has apparently revealed that Teilhard de Chardin, Jesuit and much-quoted writer on evolution and religion, is now burning in hell, while President John F. Kennedy is in purgatory because of his mishandling of the Cuban missile crisis. It is also remarkable that in an age of space travel we suddenly get extraterrestrial spirits talking to us. The point I am making is a simple one. Most of the so-called mediums or channellers are, consciously or subconsciously, simply projecting their own ideas through the medium of a supposed spirit. However, as the brief glance through history has shown, it is just possible that some revelations may either be from a divine source, or contain sufficiently significant insights to enable them to alter history - as did the Old Testament prophets, the Qur'an and Shang Ch'ing scriptures.

The question arises - how can you tell the 'genuine' and 'important' from the fraudulent or peripheral? I suppose one criterion is does the message have a consistency and pose a challenge?

In other words, beware of comforting messages which tell you what you want to hear. Pay attention to radical critiques; challenges to self-satisfaction and to the status quo. The more uncomfortable the message, the more significant it is likely to be.

I must say I also like Corinne McLaughlin's article on 'How to Evaluate Channelling'. Corinne is herself much associated with the New Age, so she is writing from within: 'Also, why should it be just because Aunt Sally is dead that suddenly she is any wiser than when she was living? If we didn't take her advice when she was living, why take it when she's dead and wanting to deliver a message as a spirit guide?'[1]

On the edges of Christianity, you can find a similar phenomenon to channelling. It is called glossolalia. It is the action of 'speaking in tongues', accounts of which appear in the New Testament, but against which St Paul writes a warning that it is a very minor 'gift of the Holy Spirit'. Yet in some circles within the churches, glossolalia has become a sign of a true faith in Christ and a sign of a superior relationship with God. The stages of glossolalia are very similar to those of mediumship. Namely, the person involved goes into a trance, or trance-like state, often through the repetitive chanting of some phrase or the singing of a refrain over and over again. Some then deliver their message, which is almost always in a language unfamiliar to the individual, but which is translated by someone else in the congregation. Occasionally, the person goes into an ecstatic state, even to the point of having to be physically restrained. The messages which come through such experiences vary enormously, from the utterly banal to what I can only describe as pseudo-biblical. This is an interesting facet of both glossolalia and of channelling: many of the messages come in a strange form of English which can be best described as pidgin Authorised Bible English, language like 'Know you that the Lord hath spoken unto thee and that He who would speak to you is present even now'. I think people believe that if it sounds like late Elizabethan, early Stuart English, it sounds more 'divine'!

But yet again, so much of the glossolalia, like channelling, is self-centred, petty and increasingly caught up with material benefits, personal development or platitudes. If there are beings trying to communicate with us, why are they so boring - or to put it another way, why are they so interested in such minor details as people's health, wealth or sex life?

Both channellers/mediums and those who regularly practise glossolalia have been the subjects of extensive research. There is always great interest in the unveiling of a fraud, and the scene was set in the nineteenth century by the infamous Fox sisters. These delightful young women are often cited as the founders of modern spiritualism, for in 1848 they began to act as mediums and convinced many of the wealthy and influential of their time of their genuineness. Then, in 1888, they confessed that the whole thing had been a hoax. Investigations by psychic researchers have from time to time exposed frauds, but this has done little if anything to dissuade others from keeping going.

Likewise, various Church commissions and reports have observed that glossolalia can be the result of half-remembered languages surfacing and that although few people fake glossolalia deliberately, the group pressure, under the hypnotic influence of regular and vigorous chanting, can induce a state in which the person is highly susceptible.

Some critics of channelling claim that it is potentially dangerous. They point to the fact that murderers such as England's Yorkshire Ripper, or the killer of John Lennon, and cultural vandals such as the Australian who smashed Michelangelo's Pietà in St Peter's, Rome, all claimed to be acting under the guidance of voices, from God or from some other entity. Yet others conclude that such voices are in fact a psychological phenomenon, derived from a split personality or from the subconscious. I am wary of the claims that channelling or glossolalia is dangerous. Any belief is dangerous – look at what can happen to perfectly peaceful Buddhists and Hindus when they feel religiously and culturally threatened as in Sri Lanka, or what happens to Christians and Muslims in areas like Armenia, Azerbaijan or Yugoslavia. On the whole, channelling, mediums and glossolalia, precisely because they are platitudinous, cosy and self-assuring, are relatively harmless. Their major hallmark is an obsession with the self and with passing on vague statements about goodwill and self-affirmation. But many people need to hear this, so traumatic has been their upbringing or recent experience. Usually channellers, mediums and glossolalians point beyond their immediate message and even messenger to some greater Power. I dislike the exploitation of people's needs that accompanies so much of the New Age channelling, just as I disliked the obvious exploitation of the desperation of mothers who had lost their children, or children who had lost their parents, in the old seances of the spiritualists. Both are usually a misuse of whatever powers may exist and an abuse of people's fears and hopes. But I cannot in all honesty say that religious history shows such claims of mediumship, of revealed messages, to be without greater significance – even if for every message that has been of significance to the world, there have been tens of thousands that were not. I think Christians need to be very careful before dismissing all such claims, and at the same time, we need to be looking very carefully at those who use glossolalia within our own faith, again, not necessarily dismissing it, but certainly being cautious about it.

Past Lives, Self-Worth

Often tied in with channelling and associated practices is the idea of reincarnation. Some forms of channelling are believed to enable you to 'hear' your former self as you were in a previous existence. Again, there is nothing remotely new or epoch-making in these claims. Many of the world's oldest major faiths are founded upon a belief in reincarnation: Hinduism in most of its forms; Buddhism; the Jains and the Sikhs; all hold to various forms of the belief in reincarnation. In the West, reincarnation has long had a place within the religious thinking of many people.

One of the interesting features in the recent upsurge in interest in reincarnation is the way in which Western tinkerers with the idea have changed the traditional understanding as found in, say, Hinduism or Buddhism. For these ancient faiths, reincarnation is just a fact of life – and death – and rebirth. It is nothing to write home about and it is very rare for anyone to be able to recall any detail of a previous life. When they do, it is of the most recent ones. I have a friend who is a Hindu devotee who has decided not to marry in this incarnation. He recalls being married before and how much he enjoyed it. He intends to marry in his next incarnation. But for this incarnation he just wishes to concentrate on study of the scriptures and practice of the meditational methods of his particular group so as to achieve a higher level of rebirth next time. But for the majority of Buddhists, Hindus and so forth, the idea of being able to recall your past lives, or indeed the merit of doing so, is news. If past lives are used, it is as a meditational exercise which helps you see the need to break free from the suffering of rebirth or which reminds you of your connectedness with all life, not as a means of self-satisfaction.

Yet, in the West there is an obsession with this. People like Shirley MacLaine claim to be able to recall hundreds of their previous lives and find great satisfaction in doing so. I have always found these claims to be interesting, for it seems that people existed in societies which they know about and in which they are already interested. Egypt is always a good one; everyone seems to recall being somebody in ancient Egypt. Yet few people recollect being a peasant in China in the Warring States period, or a woman in the thirteenth-century Bantu tribes! And why is there this fascination with finding out who you were in the past? Perhaps it is yet another example of how the self-centred dimensions of contemporary Western society find an outlet. Reincarnation and the recalling of previous lives gives some people a sense of importance and self-worth in an age where so many are simply cogs in a vast corporate or urban wheel. I would contend that the 'memories' are largely fantasies projected back into the past in order to give a sense of importance to the individual. As I have said, few believers from traditionally reincarnational faiths and cultures such as India or China would recognize this self-obsessed pursuit as having much to do with their basic belief that death is succeeded by rebirth time and time again. Indeed, in all such faiths, rebirth is seen as primarily a curse, something to be suffered before release is achieved. Tens of thousands of lives have to be lived, and not many of them as human beings. The wheel of death and rebirth is considered awful and as something from which one should seek to escape. But in the West's recent interpretation it has become an ego trip down 'memory lane': we may lead ordinary, even banal lives in the twentieth century, but through reincarnation and exploring our pasts we can become exciting figures again. This really does have very little to do with reincarnation and a great deal to do with our own egotism. In the Eastern faiths, this use of past lives makes little sense. In such traditions, the sense of being part of a vast flow of lives is meant to humble and to illustrate the futility of seeking to cling to what is transient.

I am in no way attacking belief in reincarnation. As I have said, this forms a major part of some of the world's greatest religions. I personally do not believe in it, but that is my choice. What I do attack is the exploitation of a profound religious teaching for commercial and manipulative or egotistical reasons. And that is what seems to me is going on in much of the reincarnational workshops and therapy sessions. I hope it helps people to come to terms with themselves. But they would be very mistaken if they believed that what they taught and believed had much in common with the older traditions. Let me just provide one example of what I mean. As I have said, reincarnation is not a new idea for the West. In Judaism, the Hasidim believe in a certain kind of reincarnation for their most authoritative teachers. Of these, the greatest ever was Baal Shem Tov who lived in Poland during the first half of the eighteenth century. His story of a memory of a previous life is wonderful in its humility. He recalled being a sheep in the flock of the patriarch Jacob!

Crystal Energy?

From reincarnation, which while it is a serious religious teaching has been greatly trivialized by the West and the

New Age, I want to move to one of the best known fringe activities of the New Age - crystals and rocks.

A classic New Age statement about stones is this one from the advertisement section of the magazine *Common Ground*, Winter 1991, published, needless to say, in California: 'Stones hold within them the wisdom of the ages. Using gemstones in a developmental spiral system, I can access some of that wisdom for your use.'

Stones, particularly gemstones such as diamonds and rubies, and pure crystal, have long had a fascination for human beings. The role of such jewels in ceremonies such as weddings or coronations is not accidental. Certain jewels have always been associated with various virtues: hence diamonds, because of their indestructibility, have been associated with life-long commitments and with eternity. Marble has been a favourite covering for tombs, again because it is so tough and yet retains a gloss and gleam which is virtually untarnishable - a symbol of the immortal soul. So we should not be surprised by the idea that stones have a special significance; we have always given them such a role in our lives.

What is being very strongly promoted, and contains some new beliefs, is the idea that using such stones can bring about healing or peace or, as in the advertisement quoted above, access - yet again for self-centred use - to 'ancient wisdom'.

I find this very interesting, for a number of reasons. I am a great collector of fossils, rocks and stones. I have always wanted to have pieces of ancient buildings near me; I love the sense of history and of people's hopes and joys, cares and sorrows that one can feel in an ancient temple in China or in an old country church in England. Buildings often do seem to be steeped in their past. I have spent most of my life, while on walks, looking at the ground, hunting for fossils or stone age tools. By the time I was fifteen, my collection of fossils and carved pieces of cathedrals, churches and abbeys was so great, my bedroom windowsill had to be replaced because the old one collapsed under the weight. Today, as I sit in my study writing this, I can look across the room to a new collection of fossils, stone age axes, arrow heads, carved rocks and so forth. I love to handle them, to look at them and to think about their past. So I am very sympathetic to the basic idea that in handling rocks, one is handling the past and making some sort of link with it.

I do not doubt that holding an inanimate object brings a certain calm. It does not move, but it can be handled and touched and the smoothness of a crystal or the contours of a rock can be very soothing. That use of them makes perfect sense. The sort of sense that comes from someone like the actress Jill Ireland. She was advised to use pieces of quartz to aid her in meditation after a major operation. She remarked: 'I am not saying crystals cure cancer, but when you have the disease, your peace of mind is damaged as well, and that's where they work for me.' Likewise, I identify with Alan Talansky, a New York businessman who has a 600 pound quartz in his office, beautifully lit: 'When I'm in a big hassle, I turn and look at this thing that has been around for millions of years, and it makes the problems seem less.' I find that is exactly what I do with my collection of rocks. It is the gift of a longer perspective that such ancient things bring, but I also get that from old icons or statues of the Buddha which have been venerated for centuries.

I do believe that this can be taken too far, however. I am sure that holding crystals can be calming – but so is playing with prayer beads. There is nothing inherent

within a crystal that is more or less calming than playing
with wooden, marble or even gemstone prayer beads, be
they Muslim, Christian or Buddhist. Likewise, wearing
jewellery has been a delight of humanity since time
immemorial, but this doesn't mean that it puts us in
touch with ancient wisdom. I am not sure what kind of
wisdom an igneous rock is supposed to have imbibed; or
what insights have been garnered by sedimentary rock,
heaved up from a sea bottom and then weathered by the
rain. I certainly understand the sense of these rocks being
so old that humanity must appear as an absolute
irrelevance to them, but beyond this I really do not see
what wisdom they can contain.

Sadly, there is a lot of money being made from
susceptible people by the crystal sellers and users. It is
perhaps one of the least worthwhile aspects of those
ephemeral things which cluster around the title New
Age. If people have the money to spend on such things,
then fair enough. But what concerns me is the idea that
making such a purchase gives you wisdom. It is the
'take-away' mentality applied to spirituality and
frankly, the spiritual journey is a lot more demanding
and exciting than clutching a lump of crystal to your
bosom.

There are many other fringe aspects of this New Age,
as even a quick visit to fairs such as Mind-Body-Spirit in
London will show. Most are congregating around the
term New Age in order to seem modern, exciting or
relevant, when in fact they are mostly shams, cons and
harmless tricks. In a book that wants to look seriously
at the New Age there is little space for these. So I want
to finish this chapter by looking at what is again an old
idea, central within many cultures of the world, but
which has been taken up and even abused by its faddish

use in the West in recent years. This is the whole area of astrology and horoscopes.

Not in Our Stars, But in Ourselves

Astrology and horoscopes appear as significant features in the lives of many of the followers of the world's faiths. Hinduism and Buddhism, along with traditional Chinese religion, afford the horoscope a major role in personal lives. This is only to be expected, for the philosophy of these faiths is based upon belief that who and what we are now is determined by what we did in previous lives. We are, in effect, the sum total of previous actions. It is therefore perfectly logical that such a faith would lead to horoscopes and astrology because what a horoscope purports to tell you is what forces determine you and your behaviour.

In the West, astrology and horoscopes have long been a feature of the religious cultural life of Christians, Jews and Muslims. This is for the simple reason that all three faiths have always held that the universe is part of the work of God and that therefore a link exists between all aspects of creation. Furthermore, when knowledge of the stars was at a very simple level, it was assumed that they had an influence over the whole of life on earth, from the flow of the seas to the seasons. Humanity, in the pre-Renaissance/Reformation and pre-Scientific eras, saw itself as part of that greater whole, as we shall see in the next two chapters. Thus it was that every Western court had its astrologers and the casting of horoscopes had its place. It was always subordinate, however, to a central Western belief: the belief that we have free will, free choice. This is a fundamental difference between traditional Hindu belief and traditional Christian, Jewish or Muslim belief.

Yet prior to the rise of this belief in free will, there had been a strong strand of fatalism within Western thought and belief. One only has to think of the Greek tragedies in which, if you are predestined to murder your father and marry your mother, there is nothing you can do to prevent this. It was perhaps one of the most important signs of intellectual maturity when human beings began to accept responsibility for their own actions. In those faiths with a reincarnational belief, this responsibility is strongly there but spread out over a vast timescale. In the West, with its tradition of just one life, the emphasis is on using your free will well in this life in order to secure the best form of life after death as well as ensuring that you make the best of this life.

In much of the commercial pulp published as horoscopes today, this emphasis on personal responsibility has been lost. For many people, their horoscopes have become the excuse for being as they are; for not getting on in life; for failed marriages and so forth. 'I can't help it, I'm a Libra', or whatever, has become a way of avoiding responsibility for your own actions. This is a misuse of horoscopes. I have had the pleasure of translating, with Chinese colleagues, the ancient Chinese astrological and horoscope system called the Tzu Wei. What is fascinating about this system is that the Chinese and Westerners use and understand it in very different ways. In the book we spell out very clearly how horoscopes are understood in Chinese life and thought:

It is important to understand that Chinese astrology is not giving you an absolute, fixed reading. It will tell you what is likely to happen, given your eight

characters - your Heavenly Stems and Earthly
Branches - the gods on duty at a particular time and
so on. But your fortune is to a great extent in your
hands. Chinese astrology warns you what may
happen. But, within certain parameters, you can alter
your fortune. There are many stories of people
changing their fortune through acts of kindness and
compassion. [2]

What actually happened was to surprise all of us,
especially the Chinese members of the team. After the
book was published, we got enquiries from people asking
to be told exactly what to do about a marriage, about
business or work or where to go for their holidays! We
wrote to all such enquirers and pointed out that this had
nothing to do with the horoscopes. All that the Chinese
horoscopes give you is a sense of the general direction in
which your life is going, unless you decide to alter that
direction, for good or for bad.

In my discussions with serious Western astrologers,
they have all made the same point, namely, that proper
Western astrology only indicates a likely path for your
life. It does not tell you or even, really, foretell what will
happen. But this is not how many in the West have
interpreted astrology, nor, sadly, is it how many practitioners present their work. All too often, horoscopes are
seen as being determinative, so that if you are a pig in
the Chinese system, then you will be like this and this
is what will happen to you. That is not how the Chinese
would put it. Likewise, people believe and teach that if
you are a Scorpio, then this is the kind of person you
inevitably will be. Again, proper astrologers of the
Western traditions would vehemently deny this.

What I see happening is an abnegation of moral

responsibility by taking on board a fatalistic under-standing of horoscopes. This absolves people from any or much of the sense of responsibility that is taught by all major faiths. It means you can accept what you have become without having to question it or seek to be other than that. In day-to-day decisions, you can acquiesce to the greater forces that are shaping your life. The struggle to understand free will is given up for the comforts of fatalism and predetermination. This approach is not, of course, unique to the New Age. It is also found in certain types of Christianity and Judaism, where predestination means you can abandon the uncertainties of choice and free will.

I personally do not believe in astrology or horoscopes. Having worked on Chinese systems and having studied Western sun signs and the zodiac, I find nothing which convinces me in the slightest that there is any evidence to support the claims for astrology and horoscopes. However, having said that, neither do I accept the claims made by Muslims about the Qur'an nor the beliefs about reincarnation of the Buddhists. But I respect the integrity of their views within the overall philosophical and religious world-view which they teach. What disturbs me about the way horoscopes are being used in the West, and not just by the New Age - daily newspapers have long carried 'stars' columns - is that the role of horoscopes has become dissociated from any complete religious or spiritual world-view or indeed wider purpose than personal titillation or the removal of personal respon-sibility. In the past, Christian astrologers put their teachings within a wider framework. Today, most astrologers I have met, with a few very notable exceptions, have no framework within which they place their work - other than that of making money or

satisfying individuals' egos. That is not enough of a
world-view in my mind.

Perhaps that is what worries me most about so much
of the fringe material of the New Age. It is irrelevant. At
one level, this means that unless it actually does some
harm, we can take the cool detached view of William
Penn. But at another level, when there are such vital
issues to be grappled with as the fate of the environment,
world poverty and injustice, or the fact that there are so
many psychologically and physically damaged people, I
am disturbed at the irrelevance and the at times
exploitative dimensions of these fringe activities. But I
am also angered by the similar activities that go on
within Christianity: charismatic groups leaping up and
down and speaking in tongues; biblical fundamentalism
constantly looking to interpret the Bible as a literal
handbook to personal and world history; evangelical
churches with crusades against New Age music who
then engage in chanting hypnotic choruses and work
themselves up into a fervour of agitation; witch hunts
against perfectly harmless practices involving, for
example, ley lines or solstice celebrations. Perhaps it is
the sheer scale of the rethinking that is going on in the
best of New Age - social, economic, religious and
political - and the novelty of much of the language if not
the actual ideas, which frightens people into these
narrow, self-obsessed activities. I can understand that,
but it still makes me want to question the extent to
which such fringe aspects of life take up people's time,
energy and money.

So let us now turn to what I see as being the really
important changes in thinking and behaviour which are
emerging at this time and which are so often indiscriminately labelled as New Age.

Chapter 5

Body, Mind and Human Potential

In Chapters 5 and 6 I want to look at major areas in which change is happening very rapidly, in ways which it is not always easy to discern. It is in these areas, such as our human understanding of ourselves and our understanding of the rest of creation, that I see significant changes and developments taking place, both within the principal religious and cultural traditions of our world and outside them.

In this chapter I want to concentrate on our understanding of ourselves. And I want to start by looking at the issue of the relationship between body and mind.

Holistic Health

Recently I have been suffering from migraine headaches - quite often two a week. The effect of these was terrible, producing semi-paralysis down the left-hand side of my face and even extending to my left arm. Such was the pain and the resulting disruption of my life that I was driven to visit the doctor on at least three occasions. The doctor

I saw is a good friend, but the advice I received did nothing for me. He put me on powerful drugs which made me feel dreadful and which seemed to have little effect on the migraines. I felt as if I was losing control of my body and as if there was nothing to be done but bear the pain and try and get through each week as it came.

Then my sister Yan Chi and her husband came to visit. Both of them are nurses. Yan Chi is Chinese, having been adopted by my family when she was twelve. They had both returned from Hong Kong very recently, where they had been working in the health service. Drawing upon some experiences gained in Hong Kong, upon good medical knowledge and upon common sense, they saved my life - almost literally. They sat me down and went through my diet and my lifestyle. They taught me what not to eat at any cost; what to avoid if I felt vulnerable and what exercises and practices to undertake to relax the body. Within a few days of starting on this regime, I was already feeling that I had regained mastery of myself. Over the next few weeks, the incidence of migraines dropped to less than once a week and then down to roughly once a fortnight. Having regained control, I was then able to visit another doctor who also suffered from migraines, and who put me on a course of mild drug treatment, which has virtually cleared away all traces of the migraines. The relief is enormous.

I tell this story because it reflects the extent to which we have allowed ourselves to lose touch with basic common sense about treating not just the symptoms, but the whole person. While my doctor friend focused on my migraines as a problem to be killed by drugs, he ignored my lifestyle and myself. When I was forced to look at the effects of my eating habits and general lifestyle on my body in general and on my migraines in particular, I was able to begin to regain control and thus decide what drug treatment I needed. I did not reject the use of drugs, but I had to find a way of having a context, a personal sense of being in command, within which I could make use of the drugs to finish off what I had begun.

The whole theme of healing is one that many associate with the New Age. Yet healing has always been a part of all important religious systems. From Ayurvedic medicine in Hinduism to the foundation of hospitals and clinics around all major Muslim and Christian sites, health and spiritual well-being have gone hand in hand. There is nothing new about this. But we have had to rediscover a lot about healing in the last few decades. For we have been heirs to a modern development of medicine which has ignored the human and concentrated on the chemical. In doing so, we have practised reductionism on a massive and highly dangerous scale. Anything which can help restore the balance is to be welcomed.

What do I mean by reductionism? It is the belief that by studying and then treating the particular manifestation of an illness, you have dealt with the problem. Thus my friend the doctor heard me telling him about pains in the head and gave me medicine which treated just that, and only that. It is the same mentality that until very recently told women having a mastectomy that this was just an operation and not to fuss, or that saw a miscarriage as the body's convenient way of rejecting unwanted tissue; understandings of admittedly medical problems, but without any understanding of the feelings, emotions and concerns of those to whom this was happening.

The result of seeing people simply as biological and chemical functions is that a sense of treating the whole person is lost. There are countless stories told of insensitive doctors and nurses conveying life-shattering news in an entirely matter-of-fact way.

Western medicine has done amazing things. It has developed safe means for carrying out major surgery; it has developed drugs which can help alleviate pain and suffering; it has pioneered organ transplants and has invented machines which can scan the very core of your body. These are wonderful inventions and discoveries, but they are not enough. Here is an area where encounter with other traditions and cultures, especially the Indian and Chinese medical traditions, has had a major impact. It has forced us back to looking at the body as a whole, not as parts on which to perform marvels of modern engineering, chemistry or biology. The sad thing is that this basic wisdom used to be part of our own culture, but we lost it or cast it aside in a fervour of excitement for science and for the measurable and quantifiable.

In the early 1970s I worked in Hong Kong. Here, for the first time that I can recall, I met holistic medicine. I had met holistic psychiatry, but that is a story for later on (p.122f). In Hong Kong and in mainland China I was able to see doctors working, very successfully, with a range of physical, psychological, chemical, herbal and spiritual insights, in order to ensure the well-being of the patient. For China never gave up its traditional medicines such as acupuncture, moxibustion, herbal medicine, physical exercises and so forth. Mao decreed early on in the establishment of modern China that medicine should walk on two legs – one leg being that of modern, Western medicine and the other leg being that of traditional Chinese medicine and practices. China has undertaken a great many scientific explorations of traditional medicine and techniques in order to find or show the scientific basis for much of that range of ancient practices. But even where it has been unable to find or describe a scientific basis – as in the case of acupuncture – it has never hesitated to use it.

The Hospice Movement

The growth of holistic medicine and the rediscovery of herbal remedies, homoeopathy and associated traditions have been gradual. To a certain extent this knowledge was revived back in the mid-nineteenth century, with the pioneer work of Samuel Hahnemann, a German doctor who could see that many illnesses resulted from an imbalance within the body and could therefore be treated by using substances which corrected the imbalance. There is also a long and in some places unbroken line of knowledge about medicinal herbs – just think of the fact that every child knows to rub a dock leaf on a nettle sting – as well as a long history of psychological healing within all the major faiths. But until recently, these insights were not valued. Take the hospice movement as an example. Until Dame Cecily Saunders began – as a Christian – to look at the needs of the dying and their psychological, spiritual as well as physical well-being, death was seen as primarily the greatest insult to medical science. I recall my father, an Anglican priest and chaplain to the big local hospital being asked to address the doctors on the 'problem of death'. He found that the biggest problem was not the acceptance of impending death by the patient, but the fear, loathing and professional sense of failure it engendered in the patient's doctor.

Dame Cecily saw as both a highly qualified doctor, and as a Christian, the need to treat death as something worthwhile, something important and something for which you need help to prepare. From her work at St

Christopher's Hospice in London, the notion of housing and caring for people facing death, caring for them physically and spiritually, has spread worldwide. Yet she was strongly opposed by the medical fraternity when she began. Her roots lie both within conventional medicine and within the Christian belief that the physical body is not the whole person. It was this combination, if you like Western medicine walking on two legs, which helped forge the much-valued hospice movement.

The Doctor Within

In recent years, this relationship between the physical and the spiritual or mental has become a common theme. Yet it still induces great fear in some people. Roy Livesey, of the fundamentalist *New Age Bulletin*, has written a whole book attacking alternative or complementary medicine. In his view, complementary medicine and homoeopathy in particular are occult practices, directed and overseen by Satan as a way of literally entering the body of people. Nor is it just fundamentalists who are upset by the idea of holistic medicine. In the UK the British Medical Council recently published a major attack on holistic medicine.

What exactly is it that alarms people about healing? I think it is basically that we have been taught to follow a new priesthood: one that elevates scientific knowledge over experience and common sense. The new priesthood of scientists and doctors reacts just like any other entrenched ruling body when threatened on its own turf: namely it ridicules and mocks and seeks to cast the others in a poor light. The whole issue of childbirth is a classic illustration of this. Until the mid-nineteenth century, women delivered babies. Midwives were often local women who knew basic herbal remedies and who had both experience and expertise in childbirth - not least because they had been through it themselves and knew both the pain and the joy of it. But with the rise of the medical profession, men moved in. Gynaecology became, irony of ironies, an almost totally male preserve. Here, with no possibility whatsoever of first-hand experience of childbirth, men decided what was necessary. Certainly, the move away from home births to hospital births helped save many lives. But that was as much to do with hygiene, availability of suitable facilities and modern drugs as it was to do with doctors. Women were marginalized at what for the majority was the most momentous event in their lives.

Slowly, and in the face of great prejudice, the clock has begun to be turned back. Now women have gone a long way to reclaiming childbirth for themselves. Yet the priesthood - the doctors - still finds this hard to accept. For them, childbirth is the province of the hospital, and their professional skills, drugs, machinery and expertise. The struggle that many women have had to go through in order to exert their right to have their children as they wish testifies to the state of tension between the modern medical profession and the insights and common sense that are enshrined in much holistic and alternative medicine.

I think Albert Schweitzer (1875-1965), the great Christian missionary, doctor and humanist put it very well. He said, '. . . the witch doctor succeeds for the same reason that all the rest of us [doctors] succeed. Each patient carries his own doctor inside him. They come to us not knowing this truth.'[1]

Again, let me stress that there is nothing new in

holistic medicine. Rather, we have as a culture gone up a bit of a blind alley of reductionist medicine and are now reversing back down again, albeit with considerable clashing of gears en route. What has helped us has been exposure to ancient holistic medical traditions other than our own herbalist/Christian tradition, such as the Indian Ayurvedic medical tradition, Chinese traditional medicine and certain techniques and practices from shamanism. None of these could be remotely called New Age, for they have been in use for centuries. What is new is that they now encounter each other more than in the past and have helped us in the West to recover our own traditions as well as to draw in practices, prescriptions and methods from these different cultures. However, few people in the West actually subscribe to an Ayurvedic view of the human body, or to a Chinese understanding of the physiognomy of the body. What we have done is to take what works and to adapt it to fit our Western understanding of the body, mind and even spirit, in such a way as to assist us in overcoming the split which had occurred between body and mind and spirit in recent scientific medicine.

Health and the Hoaxers

This is not to deny that even in this area charlatans and quacks operate, but then so they always have. And con merchants are to be found on both sides, in the New Age and mainstream society. I was once visiting the USA and happened to turn on the television in my hotel room to encounter an evangelist healer. His style was dramatic and certainly made for riveting viewing. Various people were called up on to the stage. There, held by two large gentlemen whom one suspected of being professional bouncers, they would outline the nature of their malady. The preacher, whose name I cannot recall, would lay his hands on the person's head and pray out loud. Then he would smite them between the eyes. The effect was dramatic. The person would reel back into the arms of the bouncers looking, not surprisingly, stunned. Then he or she would be asked by the preacher if their ailment had gone. The inevitable answer was, yes! But it was not just for this reason that the show stuck in my mind. For at the very end of the programme, the preacher/healer turned to face the camera. In a low but strong voice he asked, staring me directly in the face: 'Is there anyone out there with an ailment? If so, place your afflicted part upon the TV screen', whereupon he gave a loud shout, prayed and then smacked the camera with his hand. I have to confess that I took a cloth and wiped down the screen just in case anyone had ever 'placed their afflicted parts' on it!

I have also watched ghost operations in the Philippines. In a country town, a conman was doing the rounds claiming to perform spirit surgery without making any cuts. He had a very vivid line in discourse and a lot of pig's blood for the special effects. I gathered from friends that a few weeks later he was arrested for fraud.

Then let us not forget that in early 1992 a man with no medical training was jailed after having masqueraded as a medical doctor for twenty-five years in a northern town in England. He had apparently prescribed hairwash for cancer patients and aspirins for gall bladder trouble. He had no medical background whatsoever, but even after he was revealed as a fraud and before court proceedings, people still came to him with their illnesses. Medicine and healing are, as Schweitzer observed, as much a state of mind as a science. And this has been known and exploited for good or bad since time immemorial.

Mental Illness and Individuality

But there is another area of healing which is new, even if it is rooted in fundamental Christian, Jewish, Muslim, indeed in basic religious and spiritual understandings of what we are. This is the whole area of psychological healing.

My mother first introduced me to this. She is an occupational therapist who for many years has worked with the mentally ill. In one such job she worked in a day care centre where the whole team, doctors, psychiatrists, nurses, occupational therapists and so forth, met together regularly to all discuss each patient. In this team, my mother was given as much standing as the top doctor or psychiatrist. Together they tried to understand the different aspects of the personality and part of each patient and thus tried to tailor their response to each person according to his or her needs. This meant that each patient was treated as an individual. The particularities of their history were seen as being of overriding importance, as the starting point for any help or treatment that they might need. My mother is no romantic about this. Drugs were used to calm violent patients when this was necessary. But most of the work proceeded along the lines of working with each patient through their particular problems and history.

Self-help

The growth in self-help and healing groups in recent decades has been enormous. Be it marriage guidance, child-abuse therapy, 'wounded daughters of remote fathers', women's support networks, single-parent groups or what have you, many people have tried to take greater control over their own lives and over the forces which have so often disrupted or blighted them. Again, many of these groups have not the least link with any New Age umbrella structure or concept. They are simply people, often coming from within a major religious tradition, who feel that something needs to be done or who need support from others, and who find that others have similar experiences or concerns. There have always existed such groups, but in recent decades, psychology and psychoanalysis have revealed to many of us how deeply affected we are by past experiences and by present frustrations. For instance, mothers and daughters have often found difficulties in relating to each other and this is a problem which daughters have shared with their closest friends or even with their husbands – the many 'mother-in-law' jokes reflect this tension but from the male, son-in-law perspective. Nowadays, it has become acceptable to discuss this more openly. Novels, articles and self-help books have appeared in which this friction and ways to avoid it or work through it are openly discussed. This is a good and helpful development; it is not new, but it is more in evidence than it was in the past.

Likewise, child abuse has been for me one of the most revealing areas to have opened up for discussion and healing in the last ten to fifteen years. As a child, I was completely unaware of this issue. As a teenager, I caught the odd hint of it in strained relationships between certain fathers and their daughters – but only a hint. Then I discovered that one of our closest friends had been badly abused as a child – and she came from a good, respectable, middle-class home. Finally, I can still recall the shock and horror of being told just a few years ago, by an American feminist friend, that surveys had shown that on average, one woman in three in the USA had been abused as a child, and it is now thought that up to one man in seven may have suffered in the same way.

My children are growing up aware of this fact of life. In television dramas, in magazines for young people and in the general personal advice offered at their schools, this issue is being delicately and patiently handled. The rise of self-help healing groups to allow people to talk about these experiences means that many people are now able to face what happened to them; are able to realize that it was not their fault, nor are they irredeemably condemned; and are able to try and rebalance their lives. Similar stories can be told about wife beating; about dealing with phobias such as agoraphobia or with stressful episodes within our lives such as experience of the death of a parent or child. It has now become possible to discuss what was long held as taboo, and far from it being sex, it has been many of the above issues which have been the real taboo subjects, which I suspect later generations will see as having begun to be broken and exorcised in our time. But this does not mean that these abuses will disappear. This is one of the falsehoods sometimes peddled by New Age and other groups. What it means is that, perhaps, the damage can be more easily healed and for some the cycle of victim-inflicter can be broken.

So as can be seen, there is much in the healing world that is good. The reintegration of traditional medicine and homoeopathic treatment; the rise of self-help and healing groups to deal with personal problems and scars. None of this is to do with the New Age, though it is sometimes claimed to be by those, on both sides, who want to believe in some international conspiracy or movement. However, there are a few areas where I think caution is called for, and where distinct New Age-type philosophies need to be critically examined in relationship to healing and well-being.

Human Potential and Limitation

The first of these is the Human Potential Movement. It is one thing to restore a person's sense of worth and security after traumas such as child abuse. It is quite another thing to claim that you can be whatever you want to be. It simply is not true.

There was a recent advertisement that captured the illusion inherent within this idea of being what you want to be. It was for a car hire company and showed a car zooming off into the desert landscape of Arizona. The caption was 'Now I can be whatever I want to be' – and all this through renting a car! Were that it was so easy. The idea was that the personal freedom offered by a hire car could be equated to total personal freedom. Small factors like expense, a job to pay for the car, or responsibilities at home were simply ignored.

Now a car rental advertisement that silly is easily dismissed – though presumably somebody thought it would work or he or she wouldn't have commissioned it. But often, similar claims are made in all seriousness by human potential groups. I believe we are all capable of doing and being more than we are at present. I do not, however, believe that there is some kind of divine being within trying to get out; a higher self which is longing to take over; a real 'me' that is in some way above, beyond and different from the me that is writing this, or cooking

supper tonight or worrying about why my son is late
home from school. As an activist person, I have often been
asked by certain kinds of friends about 'where the real
"you" is', as if what I am to them is in some way unreal.
I always recall the wonderful response someone once
made to this same pompous question as put to them by
R. D. Laing. The person of whom Laing asked 'Yes, but
where is the real you?' apparently replied 'Oh him! He
buggered off fifteen years ago and I haven't seen him
since'!

I am deeply suspicious of any discussion of a higher or
real self, because what exactly is it referring to? All of us
feel dissatisfied with ourselves at some time or another.
We all fall short of what we would like to be, do or achieve.
But part of growing up is a recognition not only of our own
limitations but of the limitations and weaknesses of
those around us - not least our parents and teachers. Is the
higher self the self which aspires to conquer our
shortcomings, but is thwarted? Are there, as Eric Berne
argues in his presentation of transactional analysis,[2]
three levels of the self, each of which arises to deal with
specific levels of stress or problems? Is the higher self
some particle, some aspect of the Divine, trapped within
a material body and seeking reunion with the Divine? Or
was Carl Jung right in seeing that many people who are
psychologically disturbed still seem to have a calm and
undisturbed central self which exists in the
subconscious?

The New Age writers will offer you any of these and
more. Yet what are we really talking about? One of the
dangers of such talk is that it makes a false dichotomy
between what we do and say and what we think and are.
This is false for most people because, unless we
deliberately set out to deceive, we are as much what we

do and say as what we are and think. Indeed, I think it is foolish to force these aspects apart. 'I' do not exist in a vacuum, or as John Donne put it 'No man is an island, entire of itself; every man is a piece of the Continent, a part of the main.' Who we are is as much a social, cultural, economic and political reality as is the sense in all of us of a purpose or meaning for our lives. To divorce the one from the other is to pretend that we can grow in isolation, whereas in fact we grow through interaction. Dreams of a higher self or a real me are exactly that. In my experience with those caught up in the search for their real selves, the true problem has been deep-seated unhappiness with where they are currently. If such introspection can help in breaking the impasse they have reached in their personal relationships, job prospects or social community, then fine. But if it becomes an excuse for turning inwards in order to exist in a world of self-obsession and quest, then I would contend that far from finding the real self, such people often tend to have abandoned any attempt to integrate their diverse aspects into a functioning, compromised and flawed but quintessentially human being. As I shall be exploring in the next chapter, one irony about much New Age writing and thinking is that while it often appears superficially to accept diversity, at its heart it rejects it for a greater Truth, within which all other truths have to find a place - exactly what conventional, established religion the world over tries to do and against which, supposedly, the New Age is reacting. This is what often seems to be posited by those who claim that only by finding the higher self can the diversity of what you are be reconciled. I would argue the other way. It is only through recognizing the inherent diversity of yourself that you can know yourself. The quest for the real self is a quest for an illusion. The ability to accept what I am in my different ways and to make the best use of that, to curtail, reinforce or develop yet more aspects of who I am, this it seems to me is the way to attain a deeper knowledge of oneself.

Furthermore, pursuit of the elusive self can so easily become selfish. Christ's message on that is clearly set out in the Lord's Prayer: 'Love your neighbour as yourself'. Not more than your neighbour, nor less than your neighbour. Human potential movements frequently strike me as selfish and self-obsessed. The idea of a perfectible me is an impossible one and in my experience has led to great distress amongst some who have genuinely believed that by saying or doing something they can tap into an infallible or omnipotent self. I do believe that by opening yourself to God, God can make more of you and your life than would otherwise be the case – but that is very different from the self-centred vision so much of the Human Potential Movement promotes. As I've said before, developing the 'god within' may well lead to crucifixion or struggle and pain. It is this inevitable failure to be what we wish to be that is used by some groups as a means of manipulating people. A feature of certain kinds of guru-directed groups which promise self-fulfilment and happiness is that the lives of the followers are strictly ordered and controlled. That is to say, the guru controls the individuals by setting standards they cannot achieve and then offering forms of discipline which are supposed to enable to them to overcome this very problem, but which do not, so they need yet more teaching on how to try and realize themselves – and so on. The same phenomenon is also to be found in certain fundamentalist and evangelical Christian groups. A common feature of evangelical rallies is the setting of impossible targets for prayer or Bible study for converts who have been led to believe all their troubles are now solved. Invariably, such converts fail to keep the targets set, feel guilty and are then entrapped.

I quoted earlier the phrase of St Athanasius about God becoming man that man might become God. What Athanasius meant, it seems to me, was that through the incarnation Christ showed what humanity was capable of, both in its worst aspects, the crucifixion of love, and in its best aspects, the life and example of Jesus. To a large degree, Athanasius was affirming that the human being is of worth and is therefore worthy. But he was also using a heuristic device to some degree in that by saying what he did he provokes one to think and reflect on what this apparently outrageous statement could mean. I feel that a lot of the 'God is me' and 'I am God' talk of the New Age is heuristic. It is a cry against the transcendent, remote, judgemental God which so much conventional religion, whether Christian, Jewish, Muslim, Buddhist or Hindu - they all have this aspect - has traditionally taught. I believe it is a useful phrase and by quoting Athanasius I have wanted to show that this concept is not new, nor is it unknown within the Christian tradition. But when people such as Werner Erhard of est say that the self - that is the higher self or Self - is all that really exists, I have to part company.

Self-Determination and Perpetual Change

However, there is a profound truth about how we are the creators, wittingly or unwittingly, of our own worlds within the following statement from one of the human potential groups. The Theta seminar creed reads: 'The thinker in all of us is the creator of our universe and manifests whatever it believes to be true. Within the dominion of our minds we are surely God, for we can control what we think, and what we conceive to be true becomes the truth.'[3]

This is true, but there is more. For we do indeed create entire universes and interpret reality according to our own central role - in our minds. However, we then have to live alongside millions of other people with similar dreams in their heads, all of us also existing with the faults, failures, skills, frustrations and ultimately societal constraints which also exist. To believe that simply by living out, or retreating into, the version of truth that we prefer, in order to fortify ourselves against the outside world, will mean we are fulfilled is to live in an illusion. I interpret what has happened to me through the particular coloured spectacles that make it have significance for me. Thus failure becomes a door which closed so that another door could open. But of course that is what I will have felt, unless the door which closed shut out all possibility of new directions and choice, perhaps by driving me deeper into a dependency-based religious group, or into mental illness from which one does not re-emerge. The unhappy sexual relationship that I had has taught me to be stronger and to know what I want in a relationship. But of course it has, otherwise I would not have matured. But there is a world of difference between making sense of what is happening to you so that you can preserve a sense of personal identity and dignity, and believing that what I imagine is going to happen, will thus occur. It is the difference between living creatively with what is given and with the opportunities which emerge or are created, and living in the expectation that life will go the way I want it to go. One is maturity, the other is fantasy. There seems to be a lot of immaturity and fantasy around, which is not helpful to those caught up in it. I have seen it make people bitter when the fantasy is revealed as such; resentful when their potential does not materialize; hostile when the promise of happiness and bliss fails to deliver. Nor is this just a New Age problem. Many people in conventional religions will tell you that if you accept, for instance, Jesus, Krishna, or the Buddha, you will never be unhappy again. Unfortunately, following the Way of the servant is not an easy path, and anyone who tells you otherwise is lying. There is no great religious or spiritual figure I can think of for whom the spiritual journey was not costly. So beware of those who promise heaven on earth, or who say they can help a person achieve fulfilment and happiness. There is no final, ultimate self to be found. It is being constructed and dismantled every moment of our lives through the things we do, hope for, work at, give up, suffer, enjoy and most of all experience and reflect upon. That is why it is so interesting to be alive!

A Course in Miracles

An interesting half-way house is to be found in the immensely popular *A Course in Miracles*. This text claims to be channelled, and is fascinating because it was received by Dr Helen Schucman, a research psychologist at Columbia University's School of Physicians and Surgeons in New York. No source as such is named for the text; it seems that Dr Schucman heard it within herself, though she claims it did not come from her. It is also interesting because it is an avowedly Christian text, often rejecting in a rather witty fashion some of the more faddish elements of both channelled texts and of New Age thinking. Dr Schucman is Jewish and the text at times seems to indicate that the teaching comes direct from Jesus – yet it is worded in such a way as to be quite acceptable to many Christians. At its heart is the notion of forgiveness which comes from listening not to the ego, which is fear, but to the voice of 'inner wisdom' which is love. Through forgiveness and grace, the past can be healed and become a source of inspiration. But more importantly, this enables you to draw upon the power of love to achieve what was previously impossible for you. Much of the book (which is in three sections: an opening address, a series of 365 lessons and a concluding address to teachers) is good Christian psychology, affirming and healing through the power of forgiveness and grace. Yet underlying it is a belief that in some way this then puts you in tune with miraculous powers which can assist you to fulfilment.

Fortunately the book seems to be capable of even having a laugh at itself and thus avoids some of the pomposity of other supposedly channelled texts. Like much within the upsurge of healing and holistic care, *A Course in Miracles* addresses basic human anxieties and offers a way through these, but in the end begins to wander into paths of self-fulfilment which leave me just a little concerned as to the effect of such high hopes in a world of struggle and disappointment.

I am not sure where this upsurge of interest is leading. I believe it is having a profound effect on contemporary medicine and psychology, one that is urgently needed. I believe that most of it is helpful and important, not least because it offers ways of healing ourselves and our relationships. But I do believe there is a dangerously naive dimension which promises more than it can deliver and thus begins to wrap people in a new sense of failure and frustration.

Chapter 6

Reimagining Society

In this penultimate chapter I want to look at some of the many and diverse ideas which are currently abroad, some of which identify themselves as New Age, others of which have been claimed as such by exponents or opponents of the New Age. In the face of the major existential and material crises that are shaking us all in the West, we are responding, as we have in every such crisis, with a mixture of a return to roots, a reinterpretation of tradition, a fusion of different ideas and a synthesis between opposing ideas. We are also now in a position to draw upon a range of terminologies, symbols and expertise such as psychology, the study of different faiths and cultures and new scientific thinking in order to help us interpret and handle our experiences of the world. Although as I have argued nothing substantial has actually changed, some very interesting ways of viewing and handling reality are emerging.

Telling Our Story

I want to start with history. All telling of history is to some extent aetiological – that is, we project into the past issues and concerns of today and seek to find confirmation or affirmation for what we do today. An example is the journey of Christopher Columbus (1451-1506) to the New World in 1492. The way this story has been told over the last hundred years is fascinating. In 1892, the great debate was about science versus religion. Science was emerging as the new world force which was going to deliver utopia. Standing against it, so it was claimed, was the old culture, symbolized by religion and by Christianity in particular. So the story of Columbus was told in such a way as to heighten this debate. Columbus was pictured arguing before a special session of the Spanish Court and clergy that the world was round, while it was claimed that the clergy affirmed it was flat. Columbus became the bold scientist fighting prejudice and proving through empirical evidence – he didn't fall off the rim of the world – that he was right. The religiously narrow-minded were portrayed as seeking to block adventure, discovery and knowledge. In fact, this scene never took place and there is no evidence whatsoever that contemporary clergy or indeed anyone else in the educated classes thought the world was flat.

In 1942, Columbus had become the symbol of free people everywhere, the founder of a nation of the free which was thus able to uphold democracy and bring the torch of freedom back to a blighted, war-torn Europe. The New World was the young and upcoming force. Civilization had come with Columbus and had been transformed by the American Revolution into a new, vigorous force, which was now being brought back to a tired Europe which was in danger of losing this truth.

In 1992, Columbus had become the bogeyman. He was blamed for destroying the indigenous cultures of America; for the ecological crisis; for racism; for capitalism and so forth. All the evils of Western civilization were seen to be symbolized by him and his journey. In contrast, the indigenous people of America were presented as peaceful, living in environmental harmony and civilized beyond belief.

I would suggest that the truth about Columbus probably lies somewhere in the middle of all this, but that is not really important. Columbus is significant because we make him so. He comes to stand for trends within history which we wish, at differing times, to emphasize for political, social, religious, ideological and cultural reasons. The fact that Columbus never set foot in North America and that there were many others (Vikings, St Brendan, Bristol fishermen) who undoubtedly set foot in America before him, is irrelevant. He has become an historical figure of great significance because of what he can be seen to represent.

Subjective History and Deliberate Distortion

The role of history in the New Age and associated movements is often highly problematic and occasionally polemical. Let me give a couple of examples. The Unification Church of the Reverend Moon is seen as both part of the movement of thought and groups which constitute this elusive phenomenon called the New Age, and as a distinct religious development in its own right.

Either way, the Unification Church, arising from elements of Christianity, Korean folk religion, dualism and fuelled by anti-communist fervour, is a fascinating development of religious thought and action in the second half of the twentieth century. Moon wishes to see his Church as being the true inheritor of Christ – the true Church. Yet his reading of Old Testament stories and history and his subsequent understanding of the role and purpose of the Incarnation of Jesus are very unusual.

Moon sees history as being a clearly defined battle between good and evil. He believes that Adam and Eve were created in order to conceive perfect human beings. Unfortunately the Fall messed that up. He then sees the whole of the Old Testament as a struggle between those who wished to produce the perfect family, and the machinations of Satan which thwarted this plan; for once a perfect family had been created, it would breed and displace the rest of flawed humanity. Jesus was born to make a really determined attempt at finding the perfect woman and starting the perfect or Divine family. At the time of good being incarnate in Jesus, however, the Devil was incarnate in John the Baptist. Because John failed to acclaim Jesus as the Messiah, the Romans were able to kill Jesus thus yet again thwarting the perfect family.

This theme continues through history until – surprise, surprise – we learn that Reverend Moon takes up the mantle and is in the process of creating perfect families.

This highly unusual reading of Jewish and Christian history is of course rejected by Judaism, Christianity and Islam. Yet it provides a powerful if somewhat simplistic quasi-historical framework for interpreting the past. It also shows, to the satisfaction of believers, that they and they alone have both discovered the key to history and really understand the meaning of the Incarnation.

The second example I would give of an idiosyncratic use of history is one which has gained much media attention in Britain. David Icke is a fascinating figure: a former UK professional footballer, turned television commentator, turned Green Party spokesman, turned messiah. In his journey from the playing fields to cosmic fields, he has been caught up in the despair felt by many about the way the planet is going. In his time as a Green Party activist he wrote powerfully and illuminatingly about the environmental crisis. He always sounded apocalyptic, but then so do many within the environmental movement. But in 1990, Icke began to believe that Jesus Christ had chosen him to be the vehicle for the final message to humanity – a message about how to be reconciled with the planet. It is essential to Icke's case that he discredits the Church, for then he can claim that any attacks upon him are from an apostate Church which has failed to hear the word of God. It is also important to Icke's message that reincarnation be accepted. This leads him to write the following:

The best advice we can have in relation to reincarnation and karma was offered by Christ when he said 'Do unto others as you would have them do unto you.' That is why he said those words – to explain the workings of karma. It is reasonable to ask why, therefore, there are no direct references to all this in the Bible. The reason dates back to a meeting of the Ecumenical Church Council called by the Byzantine Emperor Justinian at Constantinople in AD 553. This council, under his direction, erased all mention of reincarnation and karma from the Bible. This was the result of Justinian's marriage to an actress called Theodora . . . . Theodora became a convert to the Monophysite beliefs, not least because if reincarnation and karma were a fact, she was going to have many problems to face in her future lives until she had learned the lessons of her actions in this one. She set about obliterating all mention of these laws in the Bible, and in doing so she believed that somehow they would no longer apply to her.[1]

There was a Council in 553, but it did none of the things claimed by Icke. Moreover, the canon and text of the Bible was formally fixed in 382, long before the date given by Icke. There is no evidence from the extant texts of the Bible, which predate 382 as manuscripts, that anything was removed. What were not included were a large number of apocryphal gospels, letters and the such like. Yet none of those that have been found and whose antiquity can be authenticated includes any mention of reincarnation. Yet this belief that Christianity suppressed reincarnation has become popular. Why? I would suggest the basic reason is that Westerners who have become attracted to reincarnation wish to feel that it has the blessing of their major religious cultural figure, Jesus Christ; they want to feel they are being faithful to him and to the teachings of God. They want reincarnation authenticated by their own model of religious authority - God, Jesus and the Bible. It is true that Origen, a second-century theologian of considerable significance, toyed with the idea of reincarnation, but he was always in a tiny minority. What is happening in the attempt to give reincarnation a form of Christian sanction is the creation of a comfort myth, which assists people in integrating a culturally alien idea into their own overall world-view.

The quotation from Icke provides an example of bad

use of history – not least because it can be easily disproved. However, the struggle for the meaning within history, and thus the reasons for our being here today, are much more serious than this. Furthermore, there is no questioning that history is generally used to make a point, except in the work of a few academics who still believe they are dealing with objective truth. The study of the use and abuse of history in the former Communist countries illustrates this. There is now a real crisis about what interpretation to place on history following the collapse of the Joachim of Fiore-influenced Marxist model of three ages.

The Third Age, or History Renewed

The particular case I want to look at is a book by Riane Eisler, an anthropologist and sociologist from California, who as an attorney and counsellor has been very involved in women's rights. Her book *The Chalice and the Blade*, published in 1987, has been called 'the most important book since Darwin's'. While this is a greatly inflated claim, her book is a very important one. I do not know if Eisler would call herself New Age. But her book is published, at least in the UK, as 'New Age/Women's Studies', so it seems fair enough to include it within the orbit of this book. However, I want to stress that I believe the book is of considerable importance way beyond the fads of the New Agers. It is symbolic to me of a whole new way of looking at history, similar to oral history or the attitude of the pioneer, and most definitely un-New Age, work of History Workshop. It is also a fine example of the sort of innovative work being done by feminist writers such as Mary Daly (for instance in her

GynEcology) and, albeit in an at times more romantic way, Caitlin Matthews or Anne Baring and Jules Cashford in their search for the Goddess.[2]

The thesis of Eisler's book is relatively simple and falls into the classic, three ages model of Joachim and into the utopia model of so much millenarian thinking. As such it is a continuum of a traditional way of viewing history. Her contention is that history has passed through two major stages and is now on the brink of a third age of unparalleled happiness and co-operation. The first age she sees as stretching from the earliest emergence of human beings until roughly the fifth millennium BC. This era she sees as being symbolized by the Chalice, a sign of sharing and of mutual care and concern, a symbol for a time in which warfare was virtually unknown and men and women lived in fundamental equality. It was not, she is swift to explain, a matriarchy. It was what she calls a 'gylany' – being a mixture of the Greek word *gyne* (woman) and *andros* (man). In other words a society in which neither ruled but both co-operated.

She then sees a new age coming around 5000 BC, when nomadic bands of Indo-Europeans began to attack this older society, which she considers existed largely in Africa, the Middle East and 'Old Europe'. The invaders conquered through the power of the Sword and they also imposed patriachy as the dominant belief and social pattern. Eisler sees the first age, the Age of the Chalice, as being further represented by the Goddess. Not as a female counterpart to the later macho gods, but as an image of fruitfulness and co-operation. With the coming of the violent, war-bringing, male-dominated Age of the Sword, the Goddess was marginalized, mocked and finally excluded. But she went underground and kept bearing witness to an alternative vision, through cults such as the Virgin Mary or Mother of God.

Finally, Eisler sees us as standing at a crisis point. The Age of the Sword, of patriarchy and dominance has brought us to the edge of self-destruction and destruction of the environment. It is now time for us to rediscover our ability to live in co-operation with each other and nature; to bring to light the Goddess as a necessary counterbalance to the God; to realize that we can live harmoniously and in balance. She sees this not as a utopian dream, but as a return to an earlier, unsullied way of life. She does not romanticize the Age of the Chalice, for life was tough and violence did occur, but it was not warfare or conquest as we know it. If we take the decision to change, Eisler believes, we can re-root ourselves in this earlier model of human existence and thus save the planet, save ourselves and live more fulfilled lives. If we can know we once lived differently, then we can break the conditioning of the Age of the Sword, which makes us think this is how it has always been, and thus will always be.

Her case is very well argued, for she asks us to remove the blinkers that we have put on and to re-view history. Her opening chapter is fascinating in that she asks us to look again at the earliest depictions we have of human beings: the great cave paintings of the palaeolithic peoples. Taking the famous caves of France and Spain, she looks at the traditional interpretations of these pictures as scenes of hunters, the hunted and of women as adjuncts to the battling, hunting activities of men. She then turns the tables by offering another way of viewing these pictures. She observes that the earliest archaeo- logists assumed that society had always been male- dominated and hunter/killing directed, thus they read the paintings according to this assumption. This also led them to interpret the figurines of heavily pregnant women, probably images of the Goddess, as symbols of early pornography! Eisler asks us to look again. She observes that women form the focus of many of the pictures; that dancing rather than hunting seems the best way of interpreting the movements on the rocks; that what have been described as weapons could be seen just as easily as trees and plants. She gives a fine example of this, citing the case of Alexander Marshack's book *The Roots of Civilisation*, where he recounts his researches into the supposed carving of a harpoon on a palaeolithic bone carving. Under the microscope he found,

that not only were the barbs of this supposed harpoon turned the wrong way but the points of the long shaft were also at the wrong end. But what did these engravings represent if they were not 'wrong way' weapons? As it turned out, the lines easily conformed to the proper angle of branches growing at the top of a long stem. In other words, these and other engravings conventionally described as 'barbed signs' or 'masculine objects' were probably nothing more than stylized representations of trees, branches and plants.[3]

The case is strengthened by the fact that no harpoons dating from the period of this and similar carvings have ever been found.

While I was reading this book, I was travelling in East Africa and was able to examine a variety of such ancient rock paintings, dating from the palaeolithic era. I found Eisler's case held up well. Whereas I was told that the pictures showed hunting and fighting, I found it just as easy to see them as paintings of ritual and dance. What was also interesting was that women were often depicted as larger than men and were often in the company of domestic or semi-domestic animals.

Eisler's argument is a good one. Namely, that because men from a 'macho' culture first interpreted these paintings, they did so in the light of their assumptions about what men had always done and been. Now she is asking us to reverse this: to see the paintings through the eyes of the feminist movement and peace/environmental movements. At one level, all she is doing is substituting one set of implied values for another. But much more subversively and excitingly, she is asking us to re-examine what we thought we knew; to see if another story can be told and to reflect on the extent to which we have assumed limitations to our capacities as individuals and cultures to act in radically different ways.

Eisler is influenced by Frederick Engel's use of the Joachim three ages model and cites with approval his thesis that the development and use of technologies, such as the making of bronze and then iron, brought about the 'world historical defeat of the female sex', though Eisler would broaden this and say that it was not just women who lost out, but also men in not being able to live in an equal way with women.

The second age, that of the Sword, is also well presented. I am not convinced by her arguments that until the coming of the Indo-European peoples, warfare was unknown or virtually so. She cites Crete as an example of a society with a very sophisticated level of living and culture, but with few if any signs of defensive fortifications. However, Crete is an island and seems to have been well protected by its navy. Such societies, especially if they exercise great power over the neighbouring cultures (as the Greek myths seem to indicate) do not need home defences. But that aside, she makes a convincing case for the older, gylanic societies being supplanted by the newly arrived patriarchal societies from about 5000 BC onwards.

Her account of both the suppression of the Goddess tradition and its continued existence underground is well told. It is a fairly familiar theme of many books which have influenced New Age thinkers. The idea is that once the Goddess ruled and that with her eclipse we lost touch with the vital nurturing aspect of the divine; with nature itself, still so often styled Mother Nature; and with the feminine (which is usually taken to mean gentler, more caring) aspects of our own personalities. This is a case which I think has a lot to commend it, even if it is often stated with the absoluteness once reserved for patriarchy. Eisler includes a compelling chapter on the suppression of the feminine within Greek philosophy and culture in which she draws our attention to the still just visible central role of women in, for example, Homer's *Odyssey* and the Delphic Oracle, and in their role as teachers, such as Themistoclea, the teacher of ethics to Pythagoras. But her major chapter on what she calls 'The Other Half of History' is on the Bible. Here she presents a powerful new way of looking at Jesus and at early church history. Again, she is summarizing much which has been written elsewhere, by feminists, theologians and feminist theologians, but she does so in a very interesting way.

She opens by presenting Jesus - whose symbols, the cross and the chalice, combine both aspects of her world views - as a gylanic figure. In a very thought-provoking and convincing section she looks at Jesus as someone who shocked people because he spoke about a new type of relationship between men and women, and because in his very life - and resurrection - he manifested this.

She then proceeds to look at the suppression of the feminine or gylanic tradition within Christianity, showing how during the earliest phases of the Church, as recorded in the Acts of the Apostles and in some of the early letters of Paul, women and men played an equal role. She then records the rise of misogyny and the gradual exclusion of women and their place in the Church.

Here, unlike Icke, Eisler is on strong historical grounds. Sadly, the writings of many of the Church Fathers (a significant term in itself) contain statements about women which are deeply offensive and profoundly disturbing. That they marginalized women and cut them out of all decision making is beyond question. That there is a tradition of deep fear of women amongst some traditional Christians today is witnessed by the present debate in the Church of England and elsewhere over the ordination of women. That some of the gospels that were excluded from the Canon of the New Testament by AD 382 included ones of a strongly feminist persuasion is also not doubted, though the vast majority of the gnostic gospels are actually as downgrading or ignoring of women as the Four Gospels.

Eisler makes a very interesting case for the success of Christianity. She claims that it was when it began to turn its back on the gylanic vision of Jesus that it began to become acceptable to a patriarchal society which had lost its original myths and cults and was seeking justification through a new set of myths and cults.

Her view of the effect of formal, State Christianity (she constantly bears witness to a deeper, original version of Christianity which continued in a hidden way and which was gylanic) is well captured in this statement:

The men in control of the new orthodox Church
might in ritual raise the ancient Chalice, now become
the cup of Holy Communion filled with the symbolic
blood of Christ, but in fact the Blade was once again
ascendent over all. Under the sword and fire of the
alliance of Church and ruling class fell not only
pagans, such as Mithraists, Jews or devotees of the old
mystery religions of Eleusis and Delphi, but also any
Christian who would not knuckle under and accept
their rule. They still claimed their goal was to spread
Jesus' gospel of love. But through the savagery and
horror of their holy crusades, their witch-hunts, their
Inquisition, their book burnings and people burnings,
they spread not love but the old androcratic staples of
repression, devastation and death.[4]

Eisler's basic thesis is that by looking at history in terms
not of fixed, inevitable forces, but through the eyes of
cultural transformation theory, we can re-imagine what
the future could be. This is of course true, to a certain
degree. She asks,

Is there really no way out of another – now, nuclear –
war? Is this to be the end for the cultural evolution
that began with such high hope in the age of the
goddess, when the power of the life-giving Chalice
was still supreme? Or are we now close enough to
gaining our freedom to avert that end?[5]

Eisler's belief, indeed, the actual reason for her studying
history in this way, is to argue that 'Yes', we can change
the direction in which our evolution has taken us and
return to or rediscover the significance of the symbol of
the Chalice, over against the Sword.

In her writings, Eisler fuses a fascinating array of Western cultural needs. First of all, she does present an at times very convincing case. I certainly will never view history, especially pre-history, in quite the same light. She has made me aware of the cultural blinkers that I have inherited. However, she is also a typical example of the utopian tradition within the West. Having rooted her vision in the legitimacy of it having been the true gospel of Jesus Christ; having freed us from having to view the extant Bible as solely normative, but having ensured that we still have a direct link to Christ, she paints a vision, using the classic three ages model, of a blissful future, as I quoted from her last page, in Chapter 2 (page 37).

Now she may well be right. By saying that Eisler follows a classic Western pattern of utopian planning, I am not dismissing it. I believe that we do indeed need new or renewed models of how we could live. But I also accept that any society will be flawed, strained and will have to handle violence and tension. While Eisler keeps a tension going between the model and the reality of both her Age of the Chalice and her Age of the Blade, she seems to abandon this when looking to the future. However, her reworking of history is a major piece of reconceiving the past in order to reimagine the future. I just wish she had not given up the intellectual struggle of the tension between the models which she had maintained almost until the end. It makes her final chapters smack of propaganda rather than vision. Where Eisler is absolutely right is in insisting that if we have a dynamic understanding of history, we can have a dynamic vision of what we could do. This is what marks out her book as being so important.

The search for a new understanding of history and especially for a feminist reading of history is far more

widespread and significant than the New Age movement
– though it has undoubtedly influenced the New Age.
However, a lot of feminist writing about, for instance, the
Goddess, swiftly becomes wishful thinking or moralistic
propaganda. This obscures the really significant work of
writers such as Mary Daly or the pioneering if
controversial research of Marija Gimbutas.[6] These
writers ask us to think and look again, just as Eisler does.
They only rarely fall into the trap of then trying to tell
us what to think. Unfortunately, not all who use their
material are as wise.

The issue of what sort of society we want is one which
has constantly been addressed by people down the ages.
Today, there are a variety of factors that have attained a
new or renewed significance in the quest for a vision of
the future. Many of these come from people and groups
who would dissociate themselves from any idea of being
New Age – as I do myself. However, there are particular
expressions within these fields which have a New-Ageish
tinge. I want to look at both the non-New Age ideas in
these fields as well as at some of the particular slants
which those wishing to show there is a New Age, for
whatever reason, give to these wider efforts. I want to stay
with the theme of understanding ourselves by having a
story about the past. Only this time I want to go back to
the very beginning of human history as interpreted
through stories of the Fall – or the lack of them. For the
Fall is being interestingly re-expressed in certain New
Age quarters.

Discovering Me in the One – the New Fall or the Constant Rise

Deep within the New Age lies its belief in a type or types of monism. This affects it almost as strongly as the belief in progressive evolution of both species and mind - an idea which has been picked up from the palaeontologist Jesuit priest Teilhard de Chardin (see page 150f). I want to look briefly at the tension between these two models which it seems to me is rarely acknowledged by those who wish to call themselves New Age.

Monism teaches that we are all just part of one greater reality and that we are all part, one of another. This is a belief that takes some comfort from modern theories about energy, which shows that energy is never destroyed but is constantly recycling. Monism sees us as all parts of a web, the damage to one part affecting the health of all other parts. In many ways, a modified form of monism has always been present within any religious belief system, for it posits that we have a relationship with the divine. However, monism runs into problems with the human race. It has to have a Fall from grace which can thus explain how and why human beings come to foul up their own nest, break the sense of unity with all other beings and stand at a distance to the divine - or at least try to do so. This Fall has been traditionally understood in terms of the sins of Adam and Eve in the Garden of Eden and their expulsion. While this is often not acceptable to those exploring monist ideas today, nevertheless a Fall has to occur if we are to explain why we are doing the things we are and which we know to be harmful to the whole.

Peters explains it thus:

This sense of one's self being whole and being united with the whole marks the end of an existential quest, the finding of a psychological holy grail. It seems to be something we thirst for, something we hunger for. The combining of psychology with religious metaphysics is producing a new age myth that describes the human psyche as originating in some primeval unity of body and spirit, of self and world. Then, the new age myth alleges, we fell. We fell because of the process of individuation. We left the warm symbiotic unity we once knew with our mother and our environment and entered the cold cruel world of independence, the world of separate ego consciousness. Yet we long to return. We long to overcome our individuality and experience again the wholeness we have lost. Our task is to realize the oneness of self and cosmos.[7]

The task of myth making is an exciting one, but there needs to be consistency. The New Age myth set out above by Peters captures well one side of the presentation. But there is another side of the New Age myth which cuts across this Fall. That is the myth of progressive evolution.

Teilhard de Chardin lived at the end of the 19th century, beginning of the 20th century. A Jesuit and an archaeologist, he sought in true Jesuit style to reconcile theology with the modern scientific theory of his time. In doing so he produced exciting new myths and notions for his era. He lived in a time when progress was the key word. Scientific development was unravelling and exploring mystery after mystery and creating new inventions daily, and few if any of its inherent problems were yet visible. Evolution had come to explain everything, for evolution was swiftly amalgamated with the Victorian notion of inevitable progress. Teilhard de Chardin was caught up in this. He saw humanity as maturing over the millennia. For him, the coming age would arrive when humanity made a quantum leap forward into a higher consciousness. This he saw as being all within the purpose of God and as a fulfilment of history; it was inevitable, he felt. The theology that arose from his teachings has been called process theology, meaning that it was concerned with showing how God in Christ was engaged in a process of development of the human potential.

To Chardin, it was obvious that time, which he saw as linear, was moving from primitive to sophisticated. Taking a social Darwinist perspective which saw each stage of evolution as an improvement on the previous stage (an idea now almost totally discredited),[8] he saw humanity as engaged in a similar process. Humanity, through knowledge, science and technology, was getting better and better. This vision was one held by many in his time. Then came two world wars and the emergence of the terrible legacy of industrialization and science. The dream began to go wrong. Humanity seemed to have run smack bang into its old behavioural patterns, and for all its knowledge, science and belief in progress, all that had really changed was that we had increased the scale of our destruction and our abuse of one another and of the planet. The theory of progress and evolution took a hard knock.

It is obvious that monism, with its myth of the modern version of the Fall, and the Teilhard de Chardin model of progress evolution cannot sit together. The one accepts that there is something discordant within the human being, the other does not. The one calls for a return to an earlier form of relationship – such as that posited by Eisler – the other sees the past as more primitive and the future as being progress. Yet these two views are often held together in a very clumsy or ambiguous way. Personally, I think that the monist/Fall/Eisler view of our past and its meaning for the future is the most intellectually and spiritually honest and challenging. I find the progress/social evolution ideas poor historically and impoverished spiritually; furthermore, as we saw briefly in looking at Alice Bailey's writings, which are of the progress/social evolution type, they contain a real danger of implicit or even overt racism. For social Darwinism arose initially to 'prove' that the white man, as the most advanced race, had a natural right to rule over the 'less developed', more 'primitive' black man. The idea of evolution was applied as a racist notion of superiority alongside social hierarchy, also seen to be dictated by the 'survival of the fittest' theory.[9] As has been pointed out, this same model of evolution and the supremacy of the white race functions in the writings of Bailey and others who espouse an evolutionary model in their vision of the future. In contrast, Eisler and her ilk make us question the assumption that earlier societies were simpler and necessarily more primitive.

Finally, the evolutionary model assumes that time is linear and that it goes forward. This cuts out the perspective of many of the world's faiths that time is cyclical. I would argue that the tension between the linear and the cyclical is an essential one, for a totally linear view is very determinist, while a totally cyclical view is often very fatalist.

The Religion of Ecology

These ideas about human purpose and place bring us to ecology. For reasons which I frankly find very difficult to understand, ecology is now almost always termed as 'New Age religion' by evangelicals and fundamentalists. Even quite sensible books on Christianity and ecology feel they have to have a 'warning' against the New Age dimensions of ecology. For many in the evangelical world, the challenge to a fundamentalist or rigidly traditional Protestant view of the world afforded by the environmental movements has been too uncomfortable for them. Thus it is with great glee that they dismiss ecology as New Age. In their book *What is the New Age?*, Michael Cole, Jim Graham, Tony Higton and David Lewis argue that the environment has become a new religion. Yet others claim that concern for the environment is worship of nature, which is pagan - which is then seen as being Satanic. I have been vilified in various books and magazines for being a Christian and yet also involved not only with ecology but with the ecological work of many different faiths. Because of my work with them, the whole of WWF and elements of the work of Prince Philip have been classified as 'New Age'. So what exactly is going on here?

There is no question but that ecology has become a major concern for people worldwide. This concern varies from anxiety about how we can maintain the necessary resources on the planet to fuel and expand our development and exploitation of the planet, through concern for endangered species, to a sense that we have made a fundamental mistake in our understanding of our place here on earth and that we need a new relationship with the rest of creation. These views can be found in all the major environmental organizations; in all the major faiths of the world; in many political parties, especially in the West and even in a humbled and changing Marxism. There is nothing New Age about them, for in most instances they arise from within age-old traditions and are seeking a variety of ways forward. To confuse new or renewed thinking with some apocalyptic or utopian New Age is to apply a very rigid and narrow definition which would be disowned by most of those engaged in this rethinking and action.

So why do the opponents portray ecology as New Age? Primarily because it is an issue of spirituality rather than one of re-allocation of resources. This was acknowledged by WWF in 1986 when it held the Assisi meetings and for the first time ever, environmental groups sat down with leaders of all the major faiths and with indigenous faiths and tried to see what they could learn from one another about how to care for the earth. Since then, tens of thousands of religious communities, drawing upon their own teachings and the information made available by environmental scientists, have launched their own environmental programmes. This process has not left a single faith untouched, for all of them had failed to live up to or to explore their own teachings on the environment.

But the spiritual dimension goes deeper than just the revitalization of the ancient faiths. The crisis of the environment asks fundamental questions concerning our role here on earth; what place and rights or duties does the rest of creation have, and how do we find a way forward in our relationships with the planet? This in turn drives us back into history, inwards into our understanding of ourselves and outwards into the quest for new ways of relating to nature. As such it reopens paths which Western society in particular has ignored or attempted to block for centuries. It asks us to look at creation as a whole, an approach which goes against certain forms of Christian teaching and most scientific thought, which sees us as both a part and apart from creation. It asks us to value and respect elements of nature; to restore to them some sense of the kinship of which St Francis wrote or of the integration which shamanism and certain forms of the 'pagan' religions inculcated through their practices and beliefs. This is what apparently so alarms the evangelists and fundamentalists.

In recent years, Christianity has undertaken a massive programme of self-criticism and of reformulation of certain key teachings in response to the environmental crisis. Christianity has had to face the fact that certain forms of Protestantism have taught that humanity has a right both to dominate and exploit the natural world. However, the stewardship model - that we may use but not abuse and should protect nature - also has a long Christian heritage. The Orthodox churches go further and see humanity as being here to serve the rest of creation - we are part of creation and participate in the creative process. In these explorations and renewed ways of seeing humanity's role, great discussion takes place about how to understand the obviously special place humanity has, within a more holistic view of all creation. This greatly alarms some 'traditional' Christians.

They feel that any attention given to the creation must of necessity detract from the creator. Indeed, they go further. Any attention given to the creation must mean that it is attention which has diverted from the creator, thus it is worship or attention to a force opposed to the creator, namely Satan. One of the most distasteful aspects of Christian evangelism has been its denigration of other beliefs. I cited earlier how Cumbey managed to make the Buddha – 'The Enlightened One' – into Lucifer, thus 'proving' that Buddhism was Satanism. This has been done time and time again, most spectacularly in the demonization of the old god of nature, Pan.

It is echoes of this which alarm these kinds of Christians. They are right to see that the environmental movement asks Christianity to re-evaluate its understanding of nature. As we shall see in the final chapter, there are plenty of resources and traditions within the broad history of Christianity which make this perfectly possible. But the hard-liners want none of this. For them, the environment is too profoundly challenging a set of issues. Far easier just to dismiss it.

Turning to what is happening in the environmental movement, there is a very interesting struggle going on at present. On one side there are ranged many of the scientists and politicians, who believe that knowledge, facts, game reserves, game wardens, self-regulation and appeal to vested self-interest are the ways forward for the environment. On the other side, there are those who see that it is we who are the problem and that a new balance of human activity with the needs of the rest of creation has to be found, and that while facts and figures may be of help, they are not what is going to save the planet from even greater environmental degradation. In the struggle between these two views of the way forward, there are certain key ideas. The first is the holistic outlook which is such a marked feature of modern healing. For many people, the basic feeling is that we need to heal the planet and thus we need to understand our place within it as part of a vision of the whole. This has been given added impetus and scientific 'authenticity' by the Gaia hypothesis of the British scientist James Lovelock. His hypothesis is a basic one. Namely that the planet itself should be considered a living organism, which has powers of self-regeneration and protection and that it is getting close to finding humanity too great an irritant. This hypothesis, with its reality-changing vision, chimes in well with many religious teachings. It also accords with the holistic outlook. As such, Lovelock has watched with both amazement and concern as the Gaia idea has been taken up in more forms than he could ever have imagined. For some in the New Age, Gaia is the old Greek goddess, the earth. The Gaia idea thus becomes for them a rediscovery of Mother Earth worship. It has legitimated for many the idea that the earth itself should be revered. But Lovelock makes it clear that in his understanding, the earth is frankly not interested in our prayers or worship, economic plans or social programmes, or in our talk of the earth as a goddess. What the earth cares about is its own continued survival, and if this means shrugging off humanity, then so be it. One of the most challenging ideas emerging from the environmental crisis and from concepts such as Gaia is the notion that humanity really isn't that important. This poses major problems to Christianity, Judaism and Islam; it is almost inconceivable to Marxism and frankly it also stands as a major unresolved issue for those who hold the highly anthropocentric view that humanity is receiving messages from Masters about how to be a successful species. Virtually all belief systems posit a special role for humanity. Australian Aboriginal beliefs hold that by retelling and enacting the lifelines, the dreamtime, life itself is kept going. At one end of the thinking, the Gaia hypothesis says - so what? Taoism believes humanity is the pivotal point by which nature is balanced – Gaia says, irrelevant. Judaism, Christianity, Islam, the Baha'is, Marxism, capitalism and nationalism all see human salvation, redemption, and progress as being the purpose of life itself. Gaia seems to say – no! Only Buddhism and Hinduism have teachings which can absorb the hypothesis that humanity, or indeed any other current species, is irrelevant and the earth has its own self-survival at the centre of its being. Such a view raises immensely complex issues which touch to the very heart of the assumption that we are important. I suspect that the hypothesis of Gaia and its challenge to humanity's self-regard will prove to be a major issue for debate and reformulation over the next few decades.

Alongside Gaia has come a rediscovery of a sense of the sacred in the world. This has its roots in all religious traditions, but is especially clear in certain indigenous traditions. These have been greatly exaggerated by those who wish to use them in a polemical way against 'Western civilization'. The romancing of the Australian Aborigines or Native North Americans has done little to help us determine what a highly industrialized, over-populated, polluted, unjust world does about its environment. While there are important reminders of a world-view which seems to have once been widespread – a reverence for creation – this is only useful in so far as it helps us examine what do do now and how to reconceive our relationship with creation. What is true is that we cannot continue along the same path we have trodden for the last three to four hundred years: the path of the desacralizing of nature, the equation of reality with material existence and the subjugation of the rest of creation to our wants and needs. But quite how we shall emerge from this is unclear, except that it will not be with one unifying world-view.

Science as Religion: Science and Religion

Let me turn now to the relationship between religion and science. One of the key books of the New Age canon is Fritjof Capra's *The Tao of Physics* published in 1975. It is described as 'An exploration of the parallels between modern physics and Eastern mysticism'. This seminal study looks at the links between the insights of modern physics and the teachings and insights of ancient faiths, in particular Buddhisms, Hinduism and Taoism.

I am not competent to discuss the physics. I have met some scientists who claim Capra distorts and mis-represents physics in order to make a journalistic point. I have met others who say Capra has taken the major insights in modern physics and brought them to a wider public in an accessible way. I cannot judge this. What I can see, however, is a most fascinating set of issues and questions which Capra has catapulted on to the world's intellectual stage. Namely, what do the emerging and changing views of reality from science tell us about the views of reality of the major faiths? Is there in fact some sort of new synthesis between the insights of science and the insights of religion? What if science is right about theories such as the chaos theory; about the ultimate unity of all energy; about the time-space ratio. What difference does this make to our understanding of ourselves, of existence and of the divine?

In the book, Capra looks almost exclusively through the eyes of Eastern traditions. In doing so, he often takes them further than they themselves would go, but that is perfectly valid. What he ignores are the different traditions in Western religion, and in fact he sees the old physics as only tangentially a product of the religious thinking of the West - and that primarily in terms of a divine hierarchy which led scientists to look for and 'find' hierarchies in science.

In response to this, others have taken up the issue of the impact of scientific models of reality on religious models of reality. Paul Davies in his *God and the New Physics* does for the Western faiths, in particular Christianity, much of what Capra does for the Eastern faiths.

Putting it crudely, can science and religion find enough common ground in their descriptions of reality for us to begin to sense that the religious vision or model of reality is in some sense provable? If not, then what does this mean for religious models of reality? Religion and science traditionally ask very different questions: religion asks why; science asks how.

The relationship between religion and science has also been bedevilled by the supposed battle between the two. But modern historians of science and many theologian scientists have shown that this really never existed in the way it has often been portrayed in popular literature. Theologians reacted in much the same way as, for example, historians, to Darwin's theory: some agreed; some disputed; some denied. But the idea of a fundamental division between science and religion was a creation of ardent scientific popular writers in the late nineteenth century. Religious thinkers and scientists have both been in the forefront of science and while churches have sometimes been slow to absorb the significance of new discoveries, so has the rest of society.[10]

However, there is something exciting happening now. Whereas in the recent past, religious thought had to keep adapting in order to absorb new scientific ideas, now science is beginning to look into the metaphysics of religion for suitable or complementary models or images. In this sense, there is a new air to the engagement between science and religion, aided by what one can only call a certain humility which has crept into science. Far from being the saviour of humanity - as it was portrayed in the nineteenth and early twentieth centuries - science has had to come to terms with certain disturbing realities. Science has solved many problems, but has also created unprecedented environmental degradation and means of mass warfare, played with nature to make biological weapons and has as yet failed to do anything about the state of being human. In other words, science has realized it is not God and that knowledge can only be of value if rooted in a moral, ethical and spiritual context.

This combination - of new ways of thinking combined with a certain humility - is what is making the contemporary engagement between religion and science so fascinating.

I would reject claims by the New Age that this exploration is New Age. It is occurring on too vast a scale and at too many levels for that to be true. But the New Age is right in pointing to this area of exploration as being a vital one and one where new paradigms are constantly being developed, shot down, and modified. Ultimately, of course, whether science agrees with the religious vision of a person, faith or cluster of faiths, is irrelevant. Faith, by its very nature, is not about quantifiable evidence. But no one would deny that the interactions between such diverse models is an area of genuine intellectual interest, even if it is not what will make or break either science or religion.

Pluralism or Unity?

An area where there is some interesting exploration of old religious ideas is that of the encounter with other religions. The New Age movement, such as it is, is almost entirely a Western phenomenon. Indeed, so much so that Ferguson in her book *The Aquarian Conspiracy* tells us that it is essentially the latest stage of the American Revolution and that its real heart and fountain spring of inspiration is the American dream, especially as it is lived out in California. This naiveté and the American smugness of her final chapters is rather disappointing, but then she seems to have had little sustained experience of any other culture. And this is a problem throughout the New Age. One of its basic assumptions is that all religions are the same and that ultimately they will all unite in one new religion. This is the old evolutionary model at work, which means that according to their understanding, Hinduism and Judaism are the most primitive religions.

But much more worrying is the way in which other religions than the Judaeo-Christian ones are used. Essentially, the New Age is uncritically Western, linear in its time model, apocalyptic or utopian in its vision of the future and individualistic in the extreme. As such it runs contrary to just about everything in the Eastern religions. We have already seen that the very belief in a new and better age is one not held by most of the Eastern faiths. Furthermore, that the evolutionary model of time and culture is one these faiths reject. What concerns me most however is that a potentially very exciting encounter between faiths is ignored for a 'pick and choose' model which simply lifts from other faiths bits that fit in with Western neuroses or angst and which ignores the more awkward issues and traditions of these faiths.

Let me illustrate this. I once worked with someone who claimed to be a kabbalist. When I enquired what she meant she told me she had read two books and gone on a week's course. When I discussed this with a Jewish colleague who was translating a major kabbalist text he threw his hands up in horror. He pointed out that in Judaism, you are not supposed even to start on the kabbala until you are forty, and that it takes years and years of devoted study to understand. Instant religious wisdom seems to have become the demand of many today; what has been rather aptly described as 'designer Buddhism'.

The great religious traditions of the world need to be listened to in detail. It requires patience and the willingness to debate. Unfortunately, the New Age often does not appear to respect the individuality of the great faiths and seems unwilling to handle their inherent diversity. It wants to lump everything together into one, amorphous mass. It is here that the theosophical input to the development of the New Age does make its mark. Let me illustrate this. Not long ago, ICOREC produced a series of books called the Essential Teaching series. Working with scholars within each tradition we produced daily readings from the scriptures of each faith, and added a commentary on why this reading was of significance within the faith. We produced volumes for Hinduism, Islam and Buddhism. Our publisher sent us the covers for the paperback versions of these three books. To our astonishment, they were labelled 'New Age'. We swiftly contacted the publisher and pointed out that if they wanted a jihad, they should keep the title 'New Age'! The assumption was that any scripture which was not Judaeo-Christian was by definition New Age. This baptism without consent into its 'fold' is one of the most distasteful aspects of the New Age. It also speaks volumes about how the great religious traditions have been reduced to their lowest common denominator or pillaged for their quirkiest most esoteric arts, in order to meet the Western spiritual hunger.

The encounter between the great religious and spiritual traditions of the world is producing profound changes and reflection. It forces us to examine what role diversity has in the world. I will discuss this further in the next chapter. Suffice it to say that, unlike the major religions in recent years, the vast majority of the New Age has failed to respond to the challenge of diversity and pluralism. Instead of exploring what diverse models of reality mean for our own models of reality, it has retreated into the self or unified all differences in a false conformity of religion. The vision of a new religion is often just part of the rejection of pluralism – a trait which lies deep in Western philosophical and religious history and one which we need to expunge.

European history is dominated by the hunt for the elusive One. This is rooted in Greek philosophical ideas that God was One, unmoveable, unaltering and omnipotent, and that all diversity was essentially subversive, ideas which also directed Greek political life. With the rise of Christianity, therefore, Europe had not only a philosophical notion that One was ultimate, but a religious understanding which, notwithstanding the Trinity, also taught that reality was One. The One could not tolerate any others, thus diversity was declared as heretical. This concept developed beyond the religious and philosophical into the political, social and economic. All major movements from Europe - Marxism, capitalism, even our insistence on our form of democracy - have had the hallmark of believing that it was *the* system for the world. The lack of interest in, understanding of or relationship with pluralism has been a major feature of the West, in marked contrast to China or India where the Ultimate is seen as diverse rather than unified.

One of the commonest New Age themes is the quest for one world religion, or for all religions to combine and become one, and it is just the same imperialist, One-obsessed drive of the West yet again. It could be argued that all these missions to convert the world to one way of thinking, believing, working, selling, and so forth have been embarked upon for the best of reasons. We have genuinely believed that it is in the best interests of people to become Christians; to have our style of democracy; to become Marxists; to have capitalism; to belong to just one religion. We genuinely believe this is for their good. But this does not stop such desires from being imperialist and insensitive to any other world view, unless it can be subordinated into our own, or so reinterpreted as to be virtually unrecognizable to its own practitioners. And we continue down this path today, with much of the more feeble thinking which goes under the name New Age; it is the desire to see everything as just variables of a Perennial Teaching or of Truth. But to claim this about traditions that have radically different models of reality is to wish for conformity at any cost, and on our terms, rather than take the risk of real diversity. And it is always our model, our terms with which we expect other religions to agree. I have lost count of the times people have told me that all religions are essentially the same. Then when they tell you what 'sameness' they see, you realize this has little to do with the religions and everything to do with the person's own wishes, hopes or beliefs.

The One still dominates, and as a culture we *know* it is for the best – even if others won't agree with us! This is the old story of Western dominance and of not wanting to handle diversity because it places such unanswerable and uncomfortable challenges to our tidy smug world.

What is interesting is that really significant new ways of thinking, such as Capra's or Eisler's, actually want to explore diversity. Capra's main point is that it is through having such diverse models as Buddhism, Hinduism and Taoism that we can begin to explore in a new way the relationship between these models, or parts of them, and the models of science. So at one level, diversity is important, at another level it is wished away. Frankly, in my view only the former is significant because I believe diversity to be a gift of God, not a terrible confusion which we have to tidy up.

There are many other areas of new thinking today. The rise of feminism, the resurgence of Islam, the growth of psychoanalysis, the questioning of all forms of world views, the collapse and reformation of Marxism – all these and more are shaping the world. Probably the most significant worldwide development is the rise of Islam, but that is another topic and because the New Age totally ignores Islam except for the Sufis, I shall not venture upon it here. In looking at the areas that I feel are most significant in the plethora of ideas, projects, programmes and events that are taking place around the world today, I have wanted to show how these stretch well beyond anything remotely describable as the New Age. They contradict certain of the assumptions of those who set themselves up as New Age gurus, and they represent a continuing debate with reality, or on what reality is, which has been going on for millennia. Finally I want to say that I do not believe we are on the edge of a new age, a third stage of human development or what have you. I believe that we are simply responding to an increase in stimuli and a growth in options which are pushing us to redefine reality in more appropriate and effective ways. This type of undertaking is not new, but perhaps the scale is unusual. It is in this that I see the excitement of our times, and not least in what this means for my faith, Christianity.

Chapter 7

'Behold I Make All Things New'

There is a revival of interest in the religious and the spiritual, yet it has largely passed the churches by. There is a great interest in the person of Jesus, yet the churches seem unable to meet this. There is a deep sense of the existence of God - variously understood - yet the churches seem unable to respond. Is it, as some have maintained, because Christianity is only part of the problem, not part of the answer? Is it because Christianity's Age is now passing? Or is it because the churches have failed to engage with the issues being raised, the hopes and fears being expressed, and in failing to engage, have simply not looked deep enough within themselves and their traditions to see if they have anything to say?

I believe it is in part all these.

Lynn White wrote a controversial article in 1967 in which he sought to identify the cultural roots of our contemporary crisis of the environment. Wishing to find the philosophy that taught us to see the world as exploitable, as being here just for our use, he firmly pointed the finger at Christianity and its offspring such as science and industrialization – both of which, he claims, were only possible because Christianity de-sacralized nature. White wrote his article in anger and in concern, for he himself is a Christian and was distressed at what he saw as Christianity's complicity in the roots of our ecological crisis. This article launched a spate of attacks on Christianity and stung some Christians into looking into these accusations. In doing so, Christians involved in the environmental movement were forced to admit that certain sections of the Christian church had indeed paved the way for the exploration of nature. Other traditions, slowly reassembled from history, from the great saints and from churches outside the Western expression of Christianity, such as the Orthodox churches or Celtic Church, showed that Christianity had as good a set of both environmental teachings and practices as any other faith. Yet these are barely acknowledged in the wider Church; only slowly are they beginning to be explored.

Has Christianity's Age passed? I don't subscribe to the three ages idea, nor do I believe we are on the edge of some new age of Aquarius, the Mayan calendar or a return to gylanic society. But I do believe that an era of a certain form of Christianity is passing and giving way, slowly and painfully, to a new era. The era that is passing is the era of hierarchical, male-dominated, imperialist Christianity. The era that is emerging is – well, that is what I want to look at in this chapter.

As to whether the churches have failed to engage with the issues which concern people, yes, I believe they have failed on most scores. Much of this failure lies in an inherent conservatism, which has meant a bunker-type mentality and a refusal to contemplate the idea that the Gospel of Christ could be expressed in alternative ways.

But let me be clear. The Christianity and the churches I am talking about are the minority: Roman Catholicism and the old Protestant denominations. For around the world, Christianity is now overwhelmingly a third world, a poor world faith. In such countries as Brazil and Argentina, South Africa and Namibia, South Korea and Sri Lanka, Christianity has developed into a myriad of new forms through indigenous churches, liberation theology, peasant theology, basic Christian communities and through interaction with the other faiths of their area. From this Christianity is emerging dramatic new ways of telling and living the Gospel. Meanwhile, with the collapse of Communism, the Orthodox and Monophysite churches are re-emerging, with their deep spirituality, folk wisdom and mysticism.

What is needed now is a retelling of the stories of Christianity in order that a new or renewed expression of Christianity can emerge. I want to look at some of the significant issues that we have examined, issues raised in part by the claims of the New Age, and see if Christianity has a response and if so, what changes these make to the shape, form and content of the Christian faith.

Christianity and Creation

Let me start with ecology, for this is the area which I know best and which brings into play a wide range of issues.

The ecological crisis is a crisis of the mind, not of resources. The world can support us and the rest of creation, but not in the way we live now, nor under the injustices which constitute our present world economic and social order. What is driving us and much of the rest of creation to the edge is how we behave, what we think we have the right to do and our apparent inability to control ourselves.

Christianity has played a role in this crisis of the mind. For by a judicious misreading of the Old Testament, we were able to convince ourselves in the late Middle Ages, and even more firmly from the Reformation onwards, that creation had been made for us to dominate and thus exploit. Yet Christianity had previously played a vital role in bringing us out of ecological crisis. The first major environmental crisis of European history was the collapse of the Roman Empire, which was the first Western society in recorded history to develop agro-business. By the fourth and fifth centuries AD, most farm land was owned and run by a very small group of businessmen. The soil was over-exploited and forests were cut down at will. Old established patterns of sustainable farming had been swept aside as the small holding farmers were bought out in a time of rocketing inflation. While the invasions of the Goths, Vandals and such like certainly didn't help, a contributory factor in the collapse of the Roman Empire – one of which most people are unaware – was environmental degradation, from the rich fields of North Africa (now the Sahara desert) to the soil erosion of the northern English hills.

Out of the economic and agricultural ruins of the Roman Empire, especially in Western Europe, came sustainable farming, forestry, lake creation and husbandry. In the sixth century AD St Benedict created the Benedictine order and established its rule of farming and meditation. His vision of farming was for the healing and creativity of the land and the succour of all its creatures. The methods of sustainable agriculture and animal husbandry that the Benedictines established in the most environmentally damaged areas of Western Europe are exactly those methods mourned by environmentalists today in the face of agro-business.

If the message of St Francis had been heeded, we would never have got into this mess in the first place. Francis has been sentimentalized into a sugary figure of a saint. But this was not the Francis who struggled to re-establish a sense of humanity being but part and parcel of the whole creation, a part of a great family. But he came too late. He came as the great campaigns against paganism were dying away after their success, and he came just as the Middle Ages began to climb up towards the deification of humanity and its products, science and industry, culminating in the revival of that most arrogant of statements, 'Man is the measure of all things.'

For there is no question but that Christianity's struggle in Western Europe, in particular with pagan gods, goddesses, beliefs and sites, marked Christianity in its attitudes to nature. The struggle resulted in the Church effectively demonizing the old deities and their associations with nature. This in turn cast a pall of suspicion over the very elements of creation – a pall which still affects some Christians, hence their fear of environmental issues. But this is not the whole story. For on the fringes of Roman Christianity there were churches and expressions of Christianity which were in tune with creation. Probably best known, and becoming even more so, is Celtic Christianity. Here, in the remote, collegiate, monastic churches of Ireland, Scotland and Wales, monks, nuns and lay people sought to live out the Christian faith in association with the wisdom they inherited from their earlier beliefs. Here creation was celebrated and humanity was seen as having a special role within God's creation, not apart from it. Here the spirituality of the monks and nuns was rooted in nature, not housed in the urban centres.

Deeply trinitarian, Celtic Christianity was also deeply nature-centred. Nowhere is this more powerfully illustrated than in the Hymn of St Patrick, a hymn sung as an invocation by which St Patrick was able to escape his persecutors who were hunting him, by being turned into a deer and thus escaping their attention. In this great hymn, Patrick invokes not only the 'strong name of the Trinity', but he also calls upon the elements of creation, such as wind, rain and fire, to protect him. He was a part of the greater creation and it was in that wider creation, that wider family of God, that Patrick saw himself standing.

Travelling east from the Celtic fringe, past Roman Christianity, which did after all throw up saints such as Benedict, Francis and Hildegard of Bingen, we come to Orthodoxy. Here, humanity was always seen as having a special role not just before God, but before all creation. For the Orthodox, from whom no industrial revolution or scientific upsurge ever came, humanity is called to be a poet, one who tells the story of all life and in telling, creates the fullness of all life. Humanity is called in Orthodoxy to be the servant of all creation, the one who offers up, like the servant priest Christ, all creation to God and through whom creation should be blessed.

This stands in strong contrast to the teachings of many Protestant groups that humanity is the purpose of creation and that therefore all else is secondary to humanity's needs. This is exemplified in the fact that the Orthodox churches in the World Council of Churches were writing and teaching about nature and creation long before any Protestant churches took up the issue and that for a long time, ecological issues were considered by many within the Protestant churches as a peripheral issue in comparison to human development and welfare.

It is important, therefore, to reclaim or rediscover the fact that the faith has always had an environmental gospel, even if it was often obliterated by the anthropocentric gospel or the hierarchical or power gospel. Many on the edges of Christianity have called for a new or transformed story of creation to be told by the Church. Writers such as Matthew Fox, Thomas Berry and Brian Swimme have argued for a new vision of creation and a new telling of the Christian understanding of the purpose of humanity.

It is important to maintain a tension, however, between this new vision of creation and the Christian tradition that has always taught that humanity has a special role in creation. That this special role has been perverted to abuse I acknowledge, but any new Christian understanding has to recognize that humanity, for better or worse, has a unique power in creation. The issue is how will or can that power be exercised for the well-being of all creation. This is the story or stories which Christianity now needs to work out. It will not be the story that the Celts would have told; it will not be the vision that St Benedict had, nor will it allow the ease with which Francis could speak of the family of creation. It will be a story or stories which will express the passion through which we have put creation, the crucifixion of nature and the resurrection which, just possibly, we could be part of. For the new story of creation will, I believe, mirror the story of the passion of Christ. Just as we now see what we did to Love when it became incarnate and lived amongst us in Jesus Christ, so we need to see that what we are doing, out of fear, greed, stupidity and arrogance, to creation is what we did to Christ. Perhaps once we make this connexion we can awake to the horror of the abuse of our power and uniqueness and be humbled enough to understand what the Orthodox mean when they call us the servants of creation.

Time and the Christian Perspective

In a way, Christianity needs also to modify its traditional theoretical view of history and time as linear, for in fact Christianity operates on a mixture of both the linear and the cyclical views of time. The traditional round of the Church's festivals, bringing certain teachings and events in the history of the faith into perspective once a year, is an important cyclical function of the Church. At the same time, the belief that Christ's passion is enacted over and over again wherever people suffer, are persecuted, ignored, brutalized or betrayed, posits a vision of time as being a fusion between the past, the present and the future, a cycle – beautifully expressed in the story of the sheep and the goats in Matthew 25:31f. In the person and experience of Christ, time stops and all is gathered in to the centre of being, the creator made created. Here is the contradiction of time and space. This collapsing of time into a fusion of the past, present and future is an aspect little explored in Christianity, yet it accords with much which we seem to be learning from studies in time and space. Meanwhile, the linear within Christianity is also important, for it tells us that just as there was a beginning of creation, so ultimately not only do we die and species die out but also the whole material world will pass one day – be it from human foolishness or from natural causes such as the sun expanding. This is important because it reminds us that all our efforts ultimately fade into insignificance against the age of a rock, the past of the planet, the extinction of species 75 million years ago by natural forces, or the sheer incomprehensible vastness of space. I feel that we need to recall both our significance as a species and our insignificance, and the linear concept of time should help us keep this in perspective, while the cyclical, re-enactment aspect of time collapsed should make us value each moment as a part of eternity.

The Divine is Plural

The challenge of religious and cultural pluralism is another force that the Christian faith has to look at and which calls for a radical reappraisal of traditional Christian ideas. Again, this is not new. While Roman Christianity had little time for any other beliefs, and indeed demonized them in order to set them outside the bounds of society, the Christianity of the Celts, of many Orthodox and of the great and geographically vast Nestorian Church tells a very different story. The richness of Celtic Christianity lies in its integration of pre-Christian Celtic beliefs and even deities, such as Brigid the goddess who became St Brigid the abbess. On the furthest eastern extremes of Christianity, Nestorian Christianity spread into China in the seventh century and through a remarkable process of translation conveyed the Gospel in terms which were entirely Chinese and yet consistent with the Gospel. Listen to this account of the purpose behind Christ's incarnation, death and resurrection. It is utterly unlike anything the early disciples would have recognized, but then so are the Creeds:

The Unique Lord, the Messiah said, 'Truly, truly I say to you, it is exactly as you say. For instance, it [the teachings] can be compared to the Precious Mountain. Its jade forests and pearl fruits, translucent and shining, sweet tasting and beautifully perfumed, can cure a person of hunger and thirst and all ills.

There was a sick man who heard of this mountain. Day and night he longed to reach this mountain and the thought never left him.

But sadly, the way was far and the mountain very high and steep. The sick man was also a hunchback and was too feeble to climb such a mountain. In vain did he try to fulfil his dream. He simply could not undertake it. But he had a near relative who was both wise and sincere. This man set up scaling ladders and had steps cut into the mountain and with others he pushed and pulled the sick man up the mountain until he reached the summit. Immediately, the sick man's illness was cured.

Know this Simon Peter, that the people who are coming to this mountain of true teachings were for a long time confused and in misery because they were burdened by their worldly passions. They had heard the truth and knew it could lead them to the Way or rest and joy - to the Mountain of Rest and Joy. They tried to reach the mountain and scale it, but in vain, for love and faith had almost died within them.'

Thereupon the Almighty Lord made himself known. He came as the near relative of the people and taught them with such skill and sincerity that they understood that he was both the scaling ladder and the stone steps by means of which they could understand the True Way and rid themselves of their burdens of confusion for ever.[1]

The Nestorians were unbound by the later theological developments of the West; Augustine and Aquinas, for example, were simply unknown to them. They took the life-giving message of Christ and found ways to express what lay at its core in language and imagery which reflected the cultures into which they went. The Celts did a similar job of celebrating the pluralism of their culture. Yet we seem to be almost incapable of doing the same.

If Christianity is to grow, it will only be through learning to see pluralism, diversity, as a God-given gift. Here we can learn from the environment. One of the key scientific insights gained as a result of the environmental crisis is the need for there to be as diverse a gene pool as possible in order to allow variety to operate and to enable evolution to continue to overcome problems and respond to crises. Hence the call by many conservation and environmental groups for the protection of what is termed 'biological diversity'. Diversity is an essential part of evolution and survival. Likewise I would argue that the God who created diversity as the way of physical growth and evolution has also provided diversity in thoughts and beliefs for much the same reason. This does not mean, however, that we thus see all diversity as equally good – or as has been the tradition, equally bad! Far from it. In biological diversity there are species which are dying out because they have not adapted; there are species being forced into extinction through abuse of the environment; there are parasitical species; there are species which pose a major threat to other species, even to life itself; there are benign species; there are species which seem to have no discernible role. The same is true in the diversity of ideas and beliefs. Some are dying out; some are arising; some are threatened by forces antithetical to them; some are parasitical; some are dangerous and so forth. Acceptance of diversity as a gift from God does not mean suspension of one's critical faculties. But it does call for a wider and greater vision of what God is doing through life and through diversity than has traditionally been the case. We need to rediscover that the divine is itself pluralist, for that surely is at heart the meaning of the Trinity.

As a Christian involved in working with other religions, ideologies and cultures I have found that there is much within my own tradition which I have had to quarry for; some things within other faiths which my own faith does not have but which have become of great importance for me in understanding and relating to the world; and points of fundamental disagreement which help to define my own understanding and vision. As a translator of ancient Chinese texts I have found that there is much within the old Chinese religious under-standings and practices which seems to me to be of vital importance for our world today and which I as a Christian wish to bring out into a stronger light and to make better known. Let me give two personal examples.

The I Ching

The I Ching was very much a cult book of the 1960s and 1970s and is often termed a 'New Age' book, which is a meaningless phrase for the oldest divination book in the world. When I tried to read it in the Wilhelm/Jung

translation I found it incomprehensible and so overlaid
with Western values, beliefs and assumptions as to be far
removed from the Chinese understanding. Sadly, the
Wilhelm edition has been the most influential, making
many people believe they are in touch with the true
Chinese wisdom. So off-putting did I find the translation
that I never gave the book much serious consideration,
especially as I knew the Chinese found the Wilhelm
translation very odd. I assumed that the difficulty lay
with the book itself.

Then I and my Chinese colleagues were asked to
translate the I Ching. We turned to Chinese practitioners
in the Far East and studied contemporary Chinese
commentaries. As I began to investigate the
understanding of the I Ching within the Chinese world,
and to translate the book itself, I began to realize that
here was a remarkable book. Remarkable because it did
not do what I think many people believe or want it to do.
It does not tell you what to do, or reveal your future. That
is not what the I Ching is about. What the I Ching is
about is the role of chance and the idea that use of a
totally random method for selecting a hexagram and line
means we have to abandon our attempts always to solve
everything through logic and reason alone. The I Ching
allows us to touch briefly the underlying flow of life, call
this God, the divine or even the flow of Nature – the
name is irrelevant. By abandoning our idea of logic we
can take the risk of hearing from some other source. The
line which the I Ching will give you will often seem
unconnected with the issue you are trying to resolve, but
by offering what is in effect a third voice, outside your
own reasoning, it helps focus your own thoughts again.
I have found the I Ching invaluable for those times when
I cannot decide what to do because the arguments seem

balanced on both sides. Into this impasse comes a
random saying from the I Ching. The result is that I am
forced to look at the problem from a different perspective.
In the end I still have to make my own decisions. People
who say the I Ching told them to do so and so are missing
the point. The I Ching never tells you anything. It simply
helps to refocus the issues with which you are grappling
and sometimes puts them in a greater context. From this
you can then proceed to make your decision.

Now as a Christian I would say that the third voice I
hear in the I Ching is the voice of God, in much the same
way that when more traditional Christians open the
Bible at random in search of guidance, they are engaging
in the same quest for a third voice. For me the I Ching
is a very important religious tool and one which I believe
fits quite easily within my world-view as given to me by
Christianity.

Taoism

Another example is rather different. I have recently been
translating some Taoist cosmic rituals. These rituals
articulate a fundamental Chinese belief that the world
is a precariously balanced set of opposites – yin and yang
– which are constantly striving to get the upper hand
against each other. The role and place of humanity is to
be the lynch pin in this balancing act. If human
behaviour veers too far towards destruction and abuse,
then one side of the forces of nature begins to get the
upper hand. It is therefore necessary for the balance to
be maintained. Through the fascinating rituals of
religious Taoism, the Taoists believe that they can retune
the universe. The effects of this belief are there to be seen

in traditional Chinese architecture, town planning and design, for these traditionally sought to strike a creative balance with the already existing forces within the land and environment.

I feel that Christianity is poor on this aspect of our relationship with the given environment. I find within the Taoist rituals I have observed and translated a great deal of wisdom and compassion and a new way of understanding our role in creation. There are hints of this within some Orthodox liturgies and teachings and indeed within the architecture of many churches we see this in practice. But we have rarely as a faith developed liturgies for the creation, liturgies which act out such an understanding both of and with the environment. I believe that the Christian faith has a lot to learn from these rituals. I do not propose that we adopt them wholesale, for we do not believe in demi-gods and baleful stars. But in our own words and ways we can learn much from the challenge of finding a way to express these notions in a Christian format. If through our prayers, services, liturgies and ritual actions we can begin to inculcate a different and dynamic understanding of our role and place within creation, our possibilities to be a reconciling force rather than a dominating force, then we may see parts of our culture begin to absorb this into the way we plan, build, farm and think. It will not 'solve' the environmental crisis overnight. But even if we do overcome the particular dimensions of this crisis through other means, we still have to rethink our place in creation per se. I believe that exploration of humanity's role as the lynch pin in creation, through ritual, can be part of this.

Disarming the Devil

This brings me to another major question with which the Christian faith has to grapple. What supernatural forces do we believe in? This is linked to an even more fundamental question which is, do we believe in the devil, in a force for evil which is in struggle and competition with God? Traditionally Christianity has believed this in various forms. It has, as I said earlier, adopted the good/evil dualism of the gnostics. But this is not what the Old Testament or Christ taught, nor is it healthy spirituality. I believe that there is no dualism, but a pluralism. I believe with the prophet Isaiah that both good and evil come from God – 'I am the Lord, there is none else; I make peace and create evil; I, the Lord, do all these things' (Isaiah 45:7) – and that belief in a devil, in a force of evil, in a struggle between cosmic forces, is a dangerous falsehood which leads us into simplistic divisions of the world between good and bad; which has allowed us to demonize anything or anyone of whom we disapprove; which has led us to see diversity as threat and thus as evil; and which ultimately stops us taking responsibility for what we do, because we can always blame someone, or something else. So for me the Church has to make a clear statement that dualism is unaccept-able, the devil does not exist and within God is to be found both good and evil, joy and suffering; as the prophet Jeremiah so powerfully put it:

Thus says the Lord;
Behold what I have built
I am breaking down,
and what I have planted
I am plucking up –

that is the whole land.
And do you seek great things
for yourself?
Seek them not;
For, behold, I am bringing evil
upon all flesh,
says the Lord,
But I will give you your life
as a prize of war in all
places to which you may go. (Jeremiah 45:4-5)

We then have to start some serious reflection on what this means for us. It means we have to abandon the idea of a big, tough daddy God who is defending us from the evil one. Instead we have to face a relationship with the diversity of God in which our response and reflection are as important as are the revelations of God which have been vouchsafed to us. It is a difficult notion and this is why it is much more tempting and much easier to slip into dualism and into a belief in an evil force. But ultimately, especially in this most bloody and terrible of centuries, we have to face the evil within us and to find a way of reconciling it with the good within us; we need to recognize that there is not just good and evil but all the grey areas in between. This is a painful process of letting go of old, frightening yet comfortably familiar models and it requires us to step out into a world of relationship with God rather than only dependence on God. It is interesting to note the thinking of radical theologians about nuclear evil, created and used by us, and the issues of evil raised by our use of such knowledge. Jim Garrison, in his book *The Darkness of God: Theology after Hiroshima*, explores this most powerfully by asking us to look at ourselves and our understanding

of God in the light of the godlike powers we have given
ourselves and which we first tried out on Hiroshima and
Nagasaki. There is, in some of the best exploratory
thinking of the New Agers, such as Spangler, a similar
attempt to reintegrate good and evil, both within
ourselves and within that reality we call God. This
reintegration is I believe, vital to our future.

Love Beyond Gender

We need to seek healing and renewal. Healing because of
the divides we have built between ourselves, between us
and the rest of creation and between the love of God and
ourselves. Much of what passes for conventional religion
is a block to this. In all major faiths, sexism and male
dominance are major blocks to our having a fuller
relationship with God. Here Eisler is so right in seeing
the damage done by the use and abuse of religion for
patriarchal ends. Some feminists, such as the theologian
Daphne Hampson, feel Christianity is irredeemably
contaminated by patriarchy. Interestingly a secular
writer such as Eisler shows that this need not be so. But
there is some major work to be done rediscovering the
feminine, the goddess, within Christianity. It is there. It
is there in the great medieval paintings of Mary as the
goddess, with Christ off at a tangent, worshipping his
Mother. It is there in the Orthodox icon of the Mother
of God's womb containing all creation; it is there in the
invocation of the female saints and in the women being
the first to whom Christ appeared after his resurrection.
It is there in so many ways, but so hidden and so needing
to be rediscovered. Ultimately it is there in the old
Shaker way of understanding the Trinity. For them, God

the creator was both Mother and Father. They understood Christ to have come to reveal the parent nature of God, both male and female, just as the Old Testament shows us the parenting, mother and father face of God's love, as in Hosea 11:1-5. Increasingly Christians are praying to God as She, as the Mother, to counterbalance the silliest idea imaginable, namely that God has a penis, that God is utterly male and can thus only be described as Father. We need a Trinity like the great Trinities of the Celts where the nature of God is as Creator, Lover, Sustainer, who through Christ and through the Spirit spreads out love to all beings. We may even need to have a quinity, in which the Mother and the Father are to be found. I believe this is what the 'Trinity' is all about. God is parent, source, sustainer and creator of all.

Perhaps for a while we need to speak of both Mother and Father, of both God and Goddess, in order to rebalance our concepts, but ultimately we need to go well beyond even Mother and Father into an understanding of love itself, as being beyond and as containing all diversity, even male and female, through which diversity love expresses itself.

I call this healing because of the great damage that has been done and is being done to men and women by the obsession of those Christians who want God to be a Man. I call this healing because through the division of the world into the good force and the evil force, we have split ourselves and made it so difficult for us to handle the good and bad and the indifferent within us. I call this healing because to encounter the Lover as God is to discover both love, forgiveness and hope. The Church has been very good at making us guilty. A sense of having fallen short is very important: it prevents us resting on our laurels and of believing that whatever we want to do is enough. It isn't, and this is where the selfishness and self-centred dimensions of what is called the New Age is worrying. God calls us to be more than that and that is costly. It may even cost us what we value most – comfort and security – but Christ was quite blunt that he had not come to bring either of those, at least not in the material sense that we normally understand. But the Christian faith needs to counterbalance its important teaching on failure and struggle with celebration.

Joy

Christianity used to be really good at celebration! In some parts of the world, notably Catholic areas such as Latin America, they still are. But a great deal of Christianity has stopped celebrating, or has so overlaid it with calls for repentance and guilt before celebration, as to have effectively killed it. In my experience, the World Council of Churches is the worst offender in this category. They are so busy being relevant and expressing shame for the past activities of certain Christians, or confessing to failure generally, that they find it almost impossible to celebrate. Yet a study of the earliest liturgies of the Church shows this was not always the case. The term 'eucharist', which is now interpreted as referring simply to the communion service, actually means praise or thanksgiving in Greek. It was a celebration of life, within which the communion service was only a part.

We need to offer again praisegiving and thanksgiving. We need to express the love of the Lover and the compassion of the Parent in order that we can be healed and learn to celebrate all that is within us and around us.

In recent years ICOREC and the WWF have pioneered Creation Festivals around the world, primarily working through churches. We have asked the churches to invite people from a wide variety of religious and secular backgrounds, especially environmentalists, to celebrate the wonders of creation and then within that to look not only at the destruction and abuse we have caused, but also at the potential for partnership between humanity and the rest of creation. This has been necessary because the environmentalists are the most guilt-ridden of the lot of us and the most pessimistic. They needed reminding that the reason why people care about creation is first and foremost because it is beautiful, wonderful and frankly mind-boggling. I believe that these Creation Festivals are the most important corporate contributions that Christianity has yet made to the environmental crisis and its resolution.

Renewal

Christianity, I believe, has the insights by which the world can most powerfully be understood. It has the vision that can lead us into a different set of relationships with each other and with creation. It has at its heart diversity and in its manifestations, variety. It is capable of transporting us with joy, of placing us at risk and of asking us to look hard at the wrongdoing and violence which we inflict on ourselves and each other. It asks us to forgive those who sin against us and it asks us to forgive ourselves in order that we may grow in self-understanding within the framework of the greater needs and purpose of all that God has created, loves and nurtures.

I do not believe that the Christianity which will draw people to this sort of understanding of themselves and of God will bear much resemblance to the Christianity currently struggling to hold on to its congregations in the West, or seeking to build defensive walls around itself as in the Bible belts. I believe that the Christianity that is emerging will lose most of its hierarchy, will be able to tell its story and the story of life in vividly different ways and will have taken on board many new ideas, shapes and forms from the diversity of faiths and cultures which it is encountering. At its heart I predict there will be a strengthened vision and understanding of the Trinity as an expression of diversity. In its worship there will be a greater sense of celebration as well as a greater sense of both the purpose of life and of the grace of God which makes life purposeful, whatsoever we poor humans may wish to think or do. It will be creation-centred, not humanity- or indeed as is often the case, man-centred. It will have shaken off most of the oppressive patriarchal thinking and behaviour that so bedevils it and it will no longer seek to split the world into God and the devil but will be exploring what it means to see all as emanating from the Trinity. This emerging Christianity will make mistakes, get things wrong, over-emphasize certain teachings or insights and hurt people en route. It will not be perfect. It will need challenging and changing itself as it becomes Tradition. It will not usher in a new age of peace, happiness and reconciliation. The gospel of Christ is as much about struggle as it is about peace. It will be flawed and foolish. But it will perhaps have learnt a few lessons and will have discarded those models of Christianity that have so restricted the gospel and the people and that have so obscured the message of reconciliation and love which Christ brought. Around this emerging Christianity, the older forms will continue for a long time. They are powerful, wealthy and established. They are familiar and comfortable, even in their oppressive manifestations. And they also carry within them the seeds of this emerging faith and thus are part of the renewal, the refocusing of Christianity.

There will be no New Age, for there has always been a new age for every generation as it comes to terms with itself and its past, present and future. There will be no utopia, no heaven on earth and I suspect there will be no Armageddon, no final war or catastrophe. Rather there will be a more faithful attempt to seek to understand what we are called to be, what mistakes we have made in the past and what possibilities for the future now lie around us. This, in my understanding, is more than enough of a reason to go on living, hoping, praying and searching. I need no new age, because Christ has always said, 'Behold I make all things new'. This was experienced as true in the past if we do but look; it can be found today, and, with God's grace, it will be found to be so in the future and the future's future. It is firm in this hope that I believe Christianity has a future and with it, perhaps even as a result of it, not only might humanity have a future - but also, God willing, all life.

Notes

Chapter 1 What is the New Age?

1 Eileen Campbell and J. H. Brennan, *The Aquarian Guide to the New Age*, The Aquarian Press, Wellingborough 1990, p. 7.

2 Marilyn Ferguson, *The Aquarian Conspiracy*, Paladin, London 1982, p. 447.

3 David Spangler, 'Defining the New Age', in *The New Age Catalogue*, 1988.

4 Ibid.

5 David Spangler, *Revelation - Birth of the New Age*, Findhorn Foundation, 1977, p. 99.

6 Marilyn Ferguson, *Brain/Mind Bulletin* 1976, quoted in *The Aquarian Conspiracy*, p. 18.

7 Fritjof Capra, *The Tao of Physics*, Wildwood House, London 1975, p. 335.

8 Constance Cumbey, *The Hidden Dangers of the*

Rainbow: The New Age Movement and our Coming Age of Barbarism, Huntingdon House, Layfayette, 1983.

Chapter 2 New Age or New Revival?

1 Norman Cohn, *The Pursuit of the Millennium*, Secker & Warburg, 1957.

2 Ibid., p. 108.

3 Riane Eisler, *The Chalice and the Blade*, Mandala, London 1990, p. 203.

4 Ted Peters, *The Cosmic Self: A Penetrating Look at Today's New Age Movements*, Harper San Francisco, 1991.

5 Jean Pierre de Caussade, *Self-Abandonment to Divine Providence*, Fontana, London 1971, pp. 91-2.

6 Martin Palmer, *Dancing to Armageddon*, Aquarian/ Thorsons, London 1992.

Chapter 3 Christ, the Antichrist and All Things New

1 Ferguson, *The Aquarian Conspiracy*.

2 Cumbey, *The Hidden Dangers of the Rainbow*, p. 17.

3 Ibid., p. 19.

4 Ibid., p. 20.

5 Ibid., p. 56.

6 Ibid., p. 136.

7 Ibid., p. 145.

8 Cumbey, *The Hidden Dangers of the Rainbow*, p. 157.

9 Roy Livesey, *Understanding the New Age*, New Wine Press, Chichester 1989, p. 33.

10 Roy Livesey, *More Understanding the New Age*, New Wine Press, Chichester 1989, p. 118.

11 John Drane, *What is the New Age saying to the Church*, Marshall Pickering, London 1991, p. 238.

12 Ibid., p. 239.

13 Peters, *The Cosmic Self*, p. 172.

14 Ibid., p. 194.

15 Ibid. p. 195.

Chapter 4 Just Because They are Dead, Doesn't Mean They are Right

1 Corinne Mclaughlin, 'How to Evaluate Channelling', in William Blood (ed.), *The New Age: An Anthology of Essential Writings*, Rider/Channel 4, London 1991, p. 53.

2 Kwok, Man-Ho, *Authentic Chinese Horoscopes*, Arrow, London 1987, p. 8.

Chapter 5 Body, Mind and Human Potential

1 Albert Schweitzer quoted in Russell Chandler,

Understanding the New Age, Word Publishing, Dallas 1988, p. 170.

2 Eric Berne, *Games People Play: The psychology of human relationships,* Penguin, Harmondsworth 1968.

3 Quoted in Peters, *The Cosmic Self,* p. 70.

Chapter 6 Reimagining Society

1 David Icke, *The Truth Vibrations,* Aquarian/ Thorsons, London 1991, p. 30.

2 Mary Daly, *GynEcology,* The Women's Press, London 1979; Caitlin Matthews, *The Elements of the Goddess,* Element, Shaftesbury 1989; Anne Baring and Jules Cashford, *The Myth of the Goddess,* Viking Arkana 1991.

3 Riane Eisler, *The Chalice and the Blade,* Mandala, London 1987, p. 5.

4 Ibid., p. 133.

5 Ibid. p. 155.

6 See especially Marija Gimbutas, *The Goddesses and Gods of Old Europe 7000-3500 BC,* University of California Press, Berkeley 1982.

7 Peters, *The Cosmic Self,* p. 61.

8 See for instance Niles Eldredge and Ian Tattersall, *The Myth of Human Evolution,* Columbia University Press, New York 1982.

9 Ibid., p. 172.

10 For those interested in exploring this area further I strongly recommend either *God and Nature*, edited by David Lindberg and Ronald Numbers, University of California Press 1986, or Arthur Peacock's *Creation and the World of Science*, Clarendon Press, Oxford 1979.

Chapter 7 'Behold I Make All Things New'

1 Author's translation of the eighth-century Chinese text of Priest Ching-ching.

Bibliography

The following books provided much of the documentary background to this book.

Bloom, William (ed.), *The New Age - An Anthology of Essential Writings*, Rider/Channel 4, London 1991

Button, John and William Bloom (eds), *The Seeker's Guide - A New Age Resource Book*, Aquarian/Thorsons, London 1992

Campbell, Eileen and J. H. Brennan, *The Aquarian Guide to the New Age*, The Aquarian Press, Wellingborough 1990

Capra, Fritjof, *The Tao of Physics*, Wildwood House, London 1975

Chandler, Russell, *Understanding the New Age*, Word Publishing, Dallas 1988

Cohn, Norman, *Pursuit of the Millennium*, Secker & Warburg, London 1957

Cole, Michael, Jim Graham, Tony Higton and David Lewis, *What is the New Age?*, Hodder & Stoughton, London 1990

The Course in Miracles, Arkana, London 1985

Cumbey, Constance, *The Hidden Dangers of the Rainbow: The New Age Movement and our Coming Age of Barbarism*, Huntingdon House, Layfayette 1983

Davies, Paul, *God and the New Physics*, J. M. Dent & Sons, London 1983

de Caussade, Jean-Pierre, *Self-Abandonment to Divine Providence*, Fontana, London 1971

Drane, John, *What is the New Age saying to the Church?*, Marshall Pickering, London 1991

Eisler, Riane, *The Chalice and the Blade*, Mandala, London 1987

Ferguson, Marilyn, *The Aquarian Conspiracy*, Paladin, London 1982

Garrison, Jim, *The Darkness of God: Theology after Hiroshima*, SCM Press, London 1982

Hunt, Dave, *Peace, Prosperity and the Coming Holocaust*, Harvest House, Oregon 1983

Icke, David, *The Truth Vibrations*, Aquarian/Thorsons, London 1991

Kwok, Man-Ho, *Authentic Chinese Horoscopes*, Arrow, London 1987

Lindberg, David and Ronald Numbers (eds), *God and*

Nature, University of California Press, Berkeley 1986

Lindsay, Hal, *The Late Great Planet Earth*, Marshall Pickering, London 1971

Livesey, Roy, *Understanding Deception*, New Wine Press, Chichester 1987

—— *Understanding Alternative Medicine*, New Wine Press, Chichester 1988

—— *Understanding the New Age*, New Wine Press, Chichester 1989

—— *More Understanding the New Age*, New Wine Press, Chichester 1989

Matrisciana, Caryl, *Gods of the New Age*, Harvest House, Oregon 1985

Pagels, Elaine, *The Gnostic Gospels*, Vintage, London 1979

Palmer, Martin, *Dancing to Armageddon*, Aquarian/ Thorsons, London 1992

—— *Elements of Taoism*, Element, Shaftesbury 1992

—— *Contemporary I Ching*, Rider, London 1989

Peacock, Arthur R., *Creation and the World of Science*, Clarendon Press, Oxford 1979

Peters, Ted, *The Cosmic Self: A Penetrating Look at Today's New Age Movements*, Harper San Francisco, 1991

Robertson, Pat, *The New Millennium*, Word Publishing, Dallas 1990

Sider, Ronald J., *Rich Christians in an Age of Hunger: a*

Biblical study, Hodder and Stoughton, London 1979

Spangler, David, *Revelation - Birth of the New Age*, Findhorn Foundation, 1977

Spink, Peter, *A Christian in the New Age*, DLT, London 1991

Swimme, Brian, *The Universe is a Green Dragon*, Bear & Co., Santa Fe, New Mexico 1984

Index

acupuncture 116-17
anthropocentrism 155-8, 171-6,
   190
Antichrist:
   coming of 24, 31, 60, 63-76,
   80
   New Age Movement seen
      as 90
apocalyptic groups 34
Aquarius, Age of 64, 170
Argüelles, Dr José 37
Aryanism 69, 71
astrology 107-10
Athanasius, Saint 45, 129
Augustine, Saint 89
authority, challenges and social
   upheaval 43-5
Ayurvedic medicine 120

Baal Shem Tov 103
Bailey, Alice Ann 68-71, 75,
   95-6, 152
behaviour change, seen as
   conspiracy evidence 72-3
Benedict, Saint 172-3
Bible:
   New Age precedents 29-31
   prophets 93-4, 96
Blavatsky, Madame Helena
   Petrova 67, 95-6
body and mind
   relationship 113-32
Brain/Mind Bulletin 21
Buddhism 38-9, 44, 107, 110
   Chinese 95

Campbell, Eileen 17,23
Capra, Fritjof 23, 159
Carey, Dr George 82
catholicity, of New Age 21
Caussade, Jean-Pierre de 46
cave paintings, re-
   interpretation 141-3
Celtic Christianity 173-4, 177,
   179
Chalice, Age of 140-1, 146
channelling 92-100, 131-2
child abuse 123-4
Chinese astrology 108-9
Chinese traditional
   medicine 116-17, 120
Chinese traditional
   religion 107, 180-3
'Christian Perfection' 47
Christianity:
   and
      astrology/horoscopes 107-8
   and creation 171-6, 190

Eastern 32, 38, 55
and the environment 169-70, 171-6, 183, 189
evangelical 80-1, 128-9, 156
evolution of 169-71, 190-1
fundamentalist *see* fundamentalist Christianity
infiltration of Church by conspirators 73-4
millenarian groups 55-6
'one' model 55
Orthodox 45, 47
and predestination 110
renewed and intellectual 26
success of 145-6
Western, new age conception 38-9
Cohn, Norman 34
communardist groups 34
Communism 37, 43
complementary medicine 118
Comte, Auguste 37
conspiracy theories 60, 62, 71-2, 76-9
creation, Christianity and 171-6, 190
Creation Festivals 189
Creme, Benjamin 63-6
crystals 104-6
cults 78
Cumbey, Constance 24-5, 62-75

Daly, Mary 139, 148
Daniel, Book of 29-30, 32, 71
Davies, Paul 160
definition, of New Age 15-16
descriptions, of New Age 17-26
Devil, the 50-1, 184-6
diversity 166
in ultimate nature of existence 52-6
under New Age label 27-8, 127
see also pluralism
Drane, John 81-2

dualism 49-52, 53, 55-6, 79, 89, 184-5

Eastern organizations 44
ecology 153-8, 171-6, 183
Eightfold Path (Peters) 83-8
Eisler, Riane 37-8, 51, 139-48, 186
'Entire Sanctification' 47
environmental programmes, religiously based 77-8, 154, 189
evolution 71-2
of Christianity 169-71, 190-1
of humanity 20
progressive, of species and mind 149, 150-2, 162
Ezekiel, Book of 93

Fall, re-expression 148-52
fantasy 130-1
fatalism 108-10
feminism, and history 147-8
Feminist Theology 54-5, 186-7
Ferguson, Marilyn 17-18, 21-2, 67, 72, 162
Fifth Buddha, the 64
Findhorn Community 18
forgiveness 132
Fox sisters 99
Francis, Saint 173
fraud 99, 120-2
free will 107-8, 110
fringe religious practices 39-42
fundamentalist Christianity:
belief in New Age Movement 25, 27, 61-2, 79-81
control of converts 128-9
on links 73

Gaia hypothesis 157-8
Garrison, Jim 185
gemstones 104
ghost operations 121
Gimbutas, Marija 148
glossolalia 98-100

gnosis 85-6
Gnosticism 35, 88-9
God, biblical portrayals 53-5
'God within us' notion 39, 45, 46-9
Goddess, the 140-2, 144, 148, 157, 186-7
Great Invocation (Bailey) 70-1
guilt 128-9, 187-9
guru-directed groups 128
gylanic societies 37|, 140-1, 144, 170

Hampson, Daphne 186
happiness, as realization of potential 48-9
Harmonic Convergence, Age of 37
healing:
  hoaxers 120-1
  holistic therapies 78-9, 113-17
  psychological 122
  self-help groups 122-4
Higher Master-dominated organizations 44
Hill, Christopher 34
Hinduism 38-9, 44, 107-8
history, idiosyncratic interpretations 134-9
Hitler, Adolf 69
holistic healing therapies 78-9, 113-17
holistic medicine 116, 118-20
homoeopathy 117, 118
horoscopes 107-10
hospice movement 117-18
human potential 45, 48-9, 84, 151
Human Potential Movement 84, 125-9
humanity, and challenge to anthropocentric views 155-8, 171-6, 190

I Ching 180-2
Icke, David 137-8

ICOREC *see* International Consultancy on Religion
Illuminati 76-7
Illuminism 77
Iman Mahdi, the 64
incarnation *see* 'God within us' notion
Incarnation of Jesus 136
International Consultancy on Religion, Education and Culture 10-11, 77-8, 189
irrelevance 111
Islam 26-7, 55, 107-8

Jesus Christ 85-6
Joachim of Fiore 32-3, 36, 38
joy 188-9
Judaism:
  and astrology/horoscopes 107-8
  dualistic world-view 50-1
  and predestination 110

Kali-yuga 39
Krishna 64
Krishnamurti 67

laser beams, in antichrist prophecy fulfilment 66-7
Lessing, Gotthold 37
Leuken, Veronica 97
Liberation Theology 54
lifestyle, effect on health 114
links, spurious 73
Livesey, Roy 62-3, 76-9, 118
Lovelock, James 157
Lucifer 73, 76, 156
Lucis Trust 68-9

McLaughlin, Corinne 97-8
Maitreya 64-5
male dominance 140-4, 186-7, 190
Manichaeans 89
Marshack, Alexander 142
Marxism 36, 37
  'one' model 55

mass hypnosis 99
Master and Teachers
    concept 68, 69, 71, 86
Matrisciana, Caryl 62
Mayan calendrical system 37,
    170
mediums 92-100
mental illness 122
messianic movements 34
Methodism 45, 46-7
millenarians, beliefs 44, 56, 64,
    140
mind *see* body and mind
    relationship
monism 149, 151-2
Monophysite Church 171
Moon, Reverend 135-6
mother/daughter
    relationships 123
Muhammad 94-5

National Socialism 44
Nayler, James 34-5, 64
Nestorian Church 32, 177-9
New Age Bulletin 76, 118
New Age Movement:
    a commercial invention 25-6
    supposed blueprint for 69, 71
    as target for opposition 25,
        27, 61-2, 79-81
    a Western phenomenon 27,
        38, 162-3
nuclear fission 185-6
numerology 7-8

occult forces 78-9, 80
'One' concept 52-6, 164-6
Orthodox Church 171, 174, 177

Paine, Thomas 36
Pan 156
patriarchy 140-4, 186-7, 190
Patrick, Saint 174
Peters, Ted 45, 83-8, 90, 149-50
physics 23, 159, 160
Plan, enforcement 65, 72, 75
Plato 52-3

pluralism:
    and Christianity 177-80
    in religious beliefs 162-6,
        184-5
Pope, the 77
potential *see* human potential
prayer beads 105-6
predestination 110
process theology 151
Prophecy, New Age Movement
    as fulfilment 66-7, 71
prophets, biblical 93×, 96
psychological healing 122
psychotechnologies 87, 88

Qur'an 94-5, 96, 110

racism 72, 152
rebirth 101-2
reductionism 115
Reformation 43
reincarnation 84-5, 101-3, 108,
    110, 137-8
religion, relationship with
    science 159-62
Renaissance 43
renewal 189-91
Revelation, Book of 30-1, 32,
    66, 71, 80
revivals *see* spiritual revivals
rocks 104-6
Roman Catholicism 45, 47
    New Age a plot of 76
Roman Christianity 173-4, 177
roots, of New Age 16

Satan 50-1
satanism 73, 75-6, 79
Saunders, Dame Cecily 117
Schucman, Dr Helen 131-2
science, relationship with
    religion 159-62
Scientology 44
self:
    diversity of 127-8
    higher or real 125-9, 131
self-determination 129-31

self-help healing groups 122-4
self-understanding 20
sexism 186-7
shamanism 120
Shang Ch'ing scriptures 94, 96
Sider, Ron 74-5
Social Darwinianism 71-2, 152
Spangler, David 18-20, 23
'speaking in tongues' 98-100
spirit surgery 121
spiritual revivals:
  current 42, 81-2, 90
  historical 35
spirituality, dependency
    model 71, 185
stewardship model (planet
    earth) 155
stones 104-6
subconscious mind 126
sublimation model for
    individuals 44-5
Sword, Age of 140-1, 143, 146
Syrian Orthodox Church 32

Taoism 23, 38-9, 182-3
  Mao Shan school 94, 96
Teilhard de Chardin, Pierre 20,
    149, 150-1
Theosophists 67, 68
three Ages model 32-3, 139,
    140
time, linearity/cyclicity
    tension 152, 162, 176-7

transactional analysis 126
Trinity 187, 190
Tzu Wei 108-9

Unification Church 44, 135-6
unity 52-6, 162-6
utopian groups 34, 35-6
utopian prophecy 36-9
utopian theories 87, 140

voices (guidance from) 99

Wei Hua-ts'un 94
Weishaupt, Adam 77
Wesley, John 46-7
White, Lynn 169-70
'witch-hunts' for
    conspirators 73
women, place in Church 145
World Council of
    Churches 188
World Wide Fund for
    Nature 77-8, 82, 154, 189
world-views:
  dualistic 50-1
  during social upheavals 43-4
  emerging 17-18
  and horoscopes 110-11

Yang Hsi 94

Zoroastrianism 50